THE
JOY *of*
PIZZA

THE JOY of PIZZA

EVERYTHING YOU NEED TO KNOW

DAN RICHER

with KATIE PARLA

Photographs by Eric Wolfinger
Illustrations by Katie Shelly

VORACIOUS
Little, Brown and Company
New York Boston London

Voracious / Little, Brown and Company
Hachette Book Group
1290 Avenue of the Americas, New York, NY 10104
littlebrown.com

First Edition: October 2021

Voracious is an imprint of Little, Brown and Company, a division of Hachette Book Group, Inc. The Voracious name and logo are trademarks of Hachette Book Group, Inc.

The publisher is not responsible for websites (or their content) that are not owned by the publisher.

The Hachette Speakers Bureau provides a wide range of authors for speaking events. To find out more, go to hachettespeakersbureau.com or call (866) 376-6591.

Photographs by Eric Wolfinger
Illustrations by Katie Shelly
Book design by Shubhani Sarkar, sarkardesignstudio.com

ISBN 978-0-316-46241-9
LCCN 2021936296

10 9 8 7 6 5 4 3 2 1

MOHN

Printed in Germany

FOR
MY MOM,
ROBIN

CONTENTS

PART 1
WHERE PIZZA BEGINS
INGREDIENTS AND HOW TO CHOOSE THEM

PART 2
TECHNIQUES

PART 3
PIZZA DOUGH RECIPES

PART 4

CLASSIC AND SEASONAL PIZZAS, SAUCES, AND CONDIMENTS

INTRODUCTION

THE JOY OF PIZZA

Pizza makes people happy. It's a universally joyful food. Aside from being absolutely delicious, it brings people together around the table to share a communal experience laced with melted cheese. It's affordable, making it accessible to all. It satisfies on a physiological level, delivering the salt, fat, and acid that our brains and taste buds crave. It's a key part of America's social fabric, with nearly 3 billion pizzas consumed annually. And pizza is a part of some of my most treasured memories, and I'd wager many of yours—from post-soccer celebrations to birthday parties.

This book is about finding even more joy in pizza by learning to make pizza well. I've spent forty years eating pizza and twenty years making it professionally, every day trying to come closer to my platonic ideal.

Truthfully, I find joy in pizza of all types—from Neapolitan to deep dish to New York–style slices. But I have landed on my absolute favorite approach to pizza. It transcends regional styles and it brings me boundless joy to share it with my friends, family, and restaurant guests, not to mention how much I love eating it myself!

I crave a rim that is crispy and deeply caramelized and that shatters when my teeth bite through it. I want the crumb (interior of the crust) to be delicate, floral scented, and flavorful with a gentle and subtle note of acidity. I love a crust with nice open holes separated by thin, pearlescent cell walls. I want toppings that are not only balanced in flavor, but sourced from farmers and food producers I have relationships with, care for, and support. If this all sounds very specific—it is! But it's where my pizza journey has taken me. Just wait till you hear about the detailed Pizza Evaluation Rubric we use every day at my restaurant, Razza, in Jersey City, New Jersey.

HOW IT STARTED

I grew up eating slices cut from big, 20-inch pies from Pizza Village in a strip mall in Aberdeen, New Jersey. Every Tuesday and Friday, my family gathered around our table for takeout. I loved opening the box, the steam and savory cheese aromas escaping as we each grabbed a slice, sharing as a family.

Pizza wasn't just a twice weekly thing for the Richers. Inevitably, sometime during the week, I would run errands with my mom, Robin, and we would pop into Pizza Village or one of the many other strip mall pizzerias on our route to grab a slice, just the two of us. We would sit in a booth beneath posters of the Amalfi Coast or the Leaning Tower of Pisa tacked to the wall and faded by the sun and time. I always ordered a plain slice and she would get the same or a Bianca or a Sicilian square slice. The pizza itself wasn't remarkable by my current standards, but the joy of those memories dwells deep inside my DNA.

Anyone who was close to their mother would look back with nostalgia on such simple, happy moments. But for me they have profound significance. Mom passed away when I was 22 years old. I was fresh out of college and just off a life changing trip to Italy with my cousin. Her death shattered me in ways I can't begin to describe, but it also gave me purpose and set me on my current path.

I had moved back home for her final days and stuck around for the long, painful year that followed. The house was dark and joyless; my father coped by withdrawing, and my older brother confronted his grief in his own way. For me, I needed something to dull the pain. I threw myself head first into learning something new: how to cook. The antidote to my grief was cooking for my dad, brother, and friends.

I became particularly obsessed (this adjective is a recurring theme in my life) with tomato sauce, determined to nail the "perfect" pasta condiment. To dial in the recipe, I channeled memories of my trip to Italy, where the sauces I had tasted were less intense and more balanced than the thick, garlic-laden, brick-hued Sunday gravy so popular in New Jersey. For a year, I practiced my sauce over and over, never satisfied and always seeking to improve on the previous batch. First I ditched the tomato paste, then reeled in the garlic, each time tweaking ingredients and proportions. I must have made it a hundred times that year.

This all-out fixation with making tomato sauce distracted me from my sadness and brought the people I loved together for the support I desperately needed. Each pot of simmering sauce allowed me small glimpses of joy in an otherwise morose time.

Only years later, with the guidance of a therapist, did I realize how my drive to repeat and improve on something as simple as a tomato sauce—and later, pizza in general—was connected in a very deep way to my mom.

Robin was a calligrapher. She spent hours each day at her workbench tirelessly practicing and perfecting her script. I remember seeing pages on her desk of the same curve being practiced over and over. There was never a day when she rested on her laurels or stopped thinking about how she could do better with the next pen stroke. Her constant pursuit of improvement is one of her greatest legacies and I honor her by approaching my craft with the same sense of dedication and near maniacal drive.

PIZZA PRACTICE

In the years that followed, I worked at random restaurants in New Jersey. At 26, I begged, borrowed, and hustled to afford a struggling pizzeria. It became an extension of my home, albeit with a repertoire that went beyond tomato sauce. That first restaurant had two wood fired ovens, so I taught myself to make pizza. The process of learning how to harness the power of flour and yeast was exhilarating and I loved feeding a sourdough starter every day—something about nurturing this living thing really appealed to me on a gut level. Making naturally leavened wood fired pizzas is not the ideal place to start if you want to really understand pizza making (what's that saying about hindsight?) and at first I was overwhelmed by the learning curve. Nevertheless, learning this new craft and bringing people together over pizza brought me an immense joy that I hadn't felt in a long time.

As I got more into pizza making, I began obsessing (told you it was a theme) over canned whole tomatoes, eager to find the brand that worked best on a pizza: its moisture level, acidity, sweetness, and flavor. Then my obsession turned to mozzarella: how to slice it, its ideal proportion to the sauce, and then how to make my own.

Pizza was no longer a single thing to me. It was the culmination of its components, each of which had its own world to understand and harness for creating a delicious final product. By the time I opened Razza Pizza Artigianale in Jersey City in 2012, I was totally consumed by the desire to not only make sauce, cheese, and dough that were better every day, but to share this experience with others.

For the past decade, my staff and I have connected daily, rolling balls of dough, trading stories, and deepening our connection to one another. We have served hundreds of thousands of pizzas, watched our young guests grow up, and

been a part of countless first dates, anniversaries, and reunions. We have become part of the community and have connected with farmers, food producers, and millers who support one another. I can't imagine anything more joyful than that.

PIZZA AT HOME

You don't need to run out and buy a pizzeria to get in on this whole constellation of joyful pizza experiences. With only a home oven, a handful of tools, and a committed curiosity, anyone can make exceptional pizza. You don't have to master wood fired baking, either (though if you do, I have some tips for that!). It's easy enough to pull out some flour, canned tomatoes, and cheese and throw together a pizza—at the very least it will be edible. But truly transcendent pizza comes from contemplating the ingredients, practicing the craft, learning from mistakes, and building on your successes.

Don't be intimidated if you've never even baked pizza before. No other food is so perfect in its imperfections, so forgiving on its way to mastery. Learning and practicing pizza making is the gift that keeps on giving—you can make a pretty good pizza with any recipe in this book, but with consistent practice your pizza can become exceptional. I highly recommend recruiting your friends and family to join you on the journey, rewarding them with pizza and all the joy it brings.

WHAT MAKES A PERFECT PIE?

My goal when making pizza, whether at Razza or in my home, is to make people happy. After all of these years of experience, I know that even mediocre pizza can spark joy—but not nearly as much as a pie that has been crafted with love and reverence for the craft. There's no such thing as the perfect pizza, of course, but that doesn't mean I can't try. Actually, it's the trial and error and the imperfections I create along the way that keep me endlessly fascinated by pizza making. A critical aspect to this lifelong quest has been the naming of my intentions. By thinking about and articulating precisely what I want each element of my pizza to feel and taste like on its own, as well as how it will work as part of a whole pie, I have been able to stay laser focused on improving my craft every day.

My goal at Razza has been to make pizza with excellent ingredients, flavorful dough, balanced high quality toppings, and an eggshell rim and sturdy structure. We don't take a single pie for granted and feel a huge responsibility to give the ingredients— from the freshly milled flour, to the hand-pulled mozzarella, to the locally grown seasonal toppings— the respect they deserve as a way to honor the millers, producers, and farmers who provide them.

The best way I know how to stay on the path for the perfect pizza is to use the Pizza Evaluation Rubric (page xviii). My staff and I created this tool to analyze each finished pizza and pinpoint how we can improve on the next. The rubric is broken down into six sections totaling nearly sixty criteria, each of which contributes to pizza perfection in our eyes.

Every day at Razza, we bake hundreds of pizzas, examining each and every one of them visually to ensure they live up to the standards of the Pizza Evaluation Rubric. It's such a part of our daily practice that we no longer bother pulling the rubric out from the binder to check off each point. Each line is etched in our minds. Obviously we don't get into the tasting part (and our customers who expect a whole pie appreciate that), but we never send a pizza out without ensuring its dimensions, build, bake, fermentation, and ingredients are up to snuff.

Some of the elements of our pizza, such as its dimensions, are guided less by personal preference than by the fact that we run a business. Our pizzas are 12 inches in diameter because we serve personal pies baked in small wood burning ovens and pizzas that size are perfect for both needs. The pizza diameter informs the rim diameter and topping area—I want the crust to be a certain fraction of the overall pizza and the toppings to mingle with the edge of the crust. We literally use a caliper (obsessive, I know, but useful!) to enforce quality control over these aspects.

The pizza should be structurally sound and the toppings should be applied with restraint and a balanced cheese to sauce ratio in mind. Other toppings should be prepared and cooked so they eat nicely and don't fall off the pizza. Managing the cheese's variables like moisture and fat content is crucial to ensure that it melts properly, and the sauce must be prepared and applied in a way that it maintains its integrity as a tomato and doesn't over-reduce in the oven to become a thick paste.

The structural integrity of our pizza is a big focus of ours and in many ways it is central to our purpose. The crust has to be strong enough to support the toppings, but it shouldn't be thick or compact. I grew up eating slices that, when you pick them up with your hands, maintain their integrity and don't droop and lose all their toppings, and I want my diners to have the same experience, albeit with higher quality, seasonal ingredients. The shaping, dough hydration (ratio of water to flour), fermentation, topping distribution, bake time, and oven temperature must all be in

balance so the final product is sturdy, not soggy. I'm looking for basically the opposite of saggy-tipped Neapolitan-style pizza that you have to eat with a fork and knife.

A properly baked pizza should be crisp but not burned, with a crust showing a nice spectrum of brown, reddish, and gray hues. The rim should be pronounced, the sauce should be velvety, and the cheese should be fully melted and on the verge of gentle browning. Assessing the bake and examining the look and color of the rim can tell us a lot about whether the dough was properly fermented. Studying the baked pizza gives a window into fermentation and can offer clues on how to improve the dough next time. A properly fermented crust will be light, with an eggshell texture that gives way to an airy crumb with the ethereal aromas of fermented wheat.

Each of these characteristics is something we have worked toward, refining our recipes and techniques to achieve them consistently. For instance, in pursuit of the ideal crust caramelization, we carefully monitor the fermentation, bake temperature, and baking time. When the tomato sauce over-reduces, we add a bit of water to the sauce for the next bake.

In the end, no matter what I like, it's what *you* like that matters. This book lays out the blueprint for my ideal pizza in the form of techniques, recipes, and the Pizza Evaluation Rubric that follows. I think you'll like the results, too. But as you grow as a pizza maker, I hope you shape your own ideal pizza, naming your own intentions for size, texture, flavor, and toppings in the elusive quest for your perfect pie.

By all accounts, pizza arrived in the United States in the late 19th century with immigrants from Italy's impoverished port towns like Naples, Bari, Genova, and Palermo, each bringing their local flatbread styles to American shores. Since then, American pizza has come a long way from its Italian origins. Of course you can find many certified authentic Neapolitan pizzerias from coast to coast. But there are also countless original styles, some unique to just a single pizza maker. My pizza falls in the latter category. I believe the key to mastering pizza is *not* to adopt an Italian American approach and import ingredients like flour, mozzarella, and tomatoes. The best pizza comes from exactly where you are, practicing with what you have at home, and finding the best ingredients in your area.

DAN'S IDEAL PIZZA

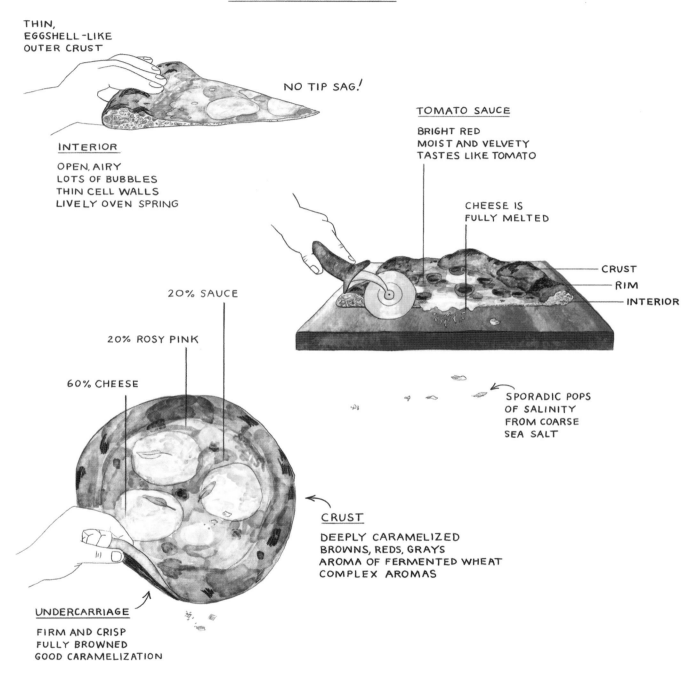

THIN,
EGGSHELL-LIKE
OUTER CRUST

NO TIP SAG!

TOMATO SAUCE

BRIGHT RED
MOIST AND VELVETY
TASTES LIKE TOMATO

CHEESE IS
FULLY MELTED

INTERIOR

OPEN, AIRY
LOTS OF BUBBLES
THIN CELL WALLS
LIVELY OVEN SPRING

CRUST
RIM
INTERIOR

20% SAUCE

20% ROSY PINK

60% CHEESE

SPORADIC POPS
OF SALINITY
FROM COARSE
SEA SALT

CRUST

DEEPLY CARAMELIZED
BROWNS, REDS, GRAYS
AROMA OF FERMENTED WHEAT
COMPLEX AROMAS

UNDERCARRIAGE

FIRM AND CRISP
FULLY BROWNED
GOOD CARAMELIZATION

PIZZA EVALUATION RUBRIC

SCAN FOR RUBRIC

To evaluate a pizza (straight from the oven), read each statement and find the numbered sentiment below that corresponds. Ideally, you want to score a 5 for each statement, a lofty goal that will keep you engaged in the process and key you in to where there's room for improvement. Be quick, as you don't want the pizza to get cold as you assess it. Scan the QR code to download and print additional rubrics.

The underlined statements apply to the round pie only.

1=Statement is not true at all
2=Statement is barely true but mostly incorrect
3=Statement is somewhat true but neutral
4=Statement is mostly true but not perfect
5=Statement is completely true and accurate

A. The Dimensions

1. ___ <u>The pizza is of the appropriate overall size, between 28 and 31 cm (11 and 12 in)</u>

2. ___ <u>Topping diameter is between 22 and 28 cm (8.5 and 11 in)</u>

3. ___ Rim diameter is between 15 and 30 mm (0.6 and 1.2 in)

4. ___ Rim height is between 15 and 30 mm (0.6 and 1.2 in)

5. ___ <u>Crust center height is between 3 and 5 mm (0.1 and 0.2 in)</u>

B. The Build

1. ___ The structural integrity is sound

2. ___ A slice can be held by the rim and stand horizontally without the point of the slice drooping downward (zero tip sag)

3. ___ The toppings are held securely on top of the crust without sliding

4. ___ The cheese to sauce ratio is appropriate. Of the topping diameter:
   a. 60 percent of the area is cheese
   b. 20 percent is tomato sauce
   c. 20 percent is a rosy, pink blend of cheese and sauce

5. ___ The sauce, cheese, and toppings are distributed evenly throughout the topping area

C. The Bake

1. ___ There is no gumline (a layer of underbaked dough beneath the sauce)

2. ___ The undercarriage is firm and crisp

3. ___ The undercarriage is fully brown with no areas of white

4. ___ The undercarriage is not burned; there are no areas of black

5. ___ The pizza can be picked up and held in the air without any bending of the structure

6. ___ There are no holes or tears in the undercarriage

7. ___ There is no ash or oven debris on the undercarriage or on top of the pizza

8. ___ The crust is not burned, charred, or black (one spot less than 2 cm is acceptable)

9. ___ The rim is deeply caramelized throughout

10. ___ Oven spring (the expansion and rising of the rim as the pizza bakes, page 108) was even and lively around the entire circumference (round) / perimeter (pan)

11. ___ The sauce is moist and velvety—not over-reduced, thick, dry, pasty, or acidic

12. ___ The cheese is completely melted, with visible areas of gentle browning

13. ___ The cheese has not broken due to overbaking (no oily puddles on top of cheese)

14. ___ There are no pools of moisture on top due to excess or underbaked toppings

15. ___ There is an audible crackling sound and feel when the slicer cuts through it

D. Fermentation

1. ____ The rim has a thin, eggshell-like outer crust and will shatter when teeth bite through it

2. ____ The crust is fully aged/mature—there are many shades of browns, reds, and grays

3. ____ The crust is not underproofed. These are the signs of underproofed dough:

   a. Thick outer crust, little to no oven spring

   b. Monotone in color

   c. Underproofed dough takes longer to caramelize in the oven leading to broken cheese and over-reduced sauce

   d. Underproofed dough does not typically spring to the desired rim dimensions

   e. Underproofed crust lacks the desired aroma and flavor

4. ____ The interior of the rim is open and airy with many (not just one or two) gas pockets

5. ____ The numerous gas pockets in the rim are separated by thin cell walls that are springy

6. ____ The texture of the interior rim is light and delicate—not tight and dense

7. ____ There is an unmistakable ethereal aroma of fermented wheat

8. ____ A perceptible yet gentle acidity is present when tasting the crust (sourdough pizza only)

9. ____ The acidity is not harsh and vinegar-like or off-putting (sourdough pizza only)

10. ____ The color of the interior rim is creamy off-white

11. ____ The color of the interior is not bright white

E. Ingredients

1. ____ The cheese is fully melted yet not broken

2. ____ The cheese will pull in a long strand when stretched

3. ____ The cheese is buttery and rich in flavor

4. ____ The cheese flows into the sauce with no clear line defining the end of the cheese and beginning of the sauce

5. ____ The tomato has a gentle acidity

6. ____ The tomato has a bright red color (not brown, rusty, or maroon)

7. ____ The texture of the tomato is accurate based on the intention

8. ____ The tomato has apparent sweetness without being cloying

9. ____ The tomato sauce tastes like a tomato

10. ____ The salt content of the tomato is appropriate—not too salty yet definitely seasoned

11. ____ There are no negative flavor attributes present in any of the toppings

12. ____ The flavor of extra-virgin olive oil is present without there being a pool of oil

13. ____ There are sporadic bites with a pop of salinity from coarse sea salt

F. Taster Opinion

1. ____ The pizza was built and baked with care

2. ____ The pizza was easy to consume without excess/mess left on the plate

3. ____ The pizza was greatly enjoyed during the moment of consumption

4. ____ The pizza left a deeply emotional and long-lasting positive impression

5. ____ The pizza was easy to digest—no feeling of lethargy or bloating

6. ____ The pizza was served at the appropriate temperature (HOT!)

7. ____ The pizza was accurately produced based on your intentions

HOW TO USE THIS BOOK

I hesitate to talk about pizza as a whole right off the bat. For me, pizza making is the product of choices: the flour you use, whether you let it rise with commercial yeast or sourdough starter, how you source toppings, and in what oven you bake your pie. I cover all those topics in the chapters that follow.

Before you get started, read through the ingredients in Part 1 so you know how to source your raw materials and how they will interact with one another. A set of ingredient rubrics will assist your sourcing. Print them and take notes using the QR codes that accompany them. Next, take a deep dive into the Techniques chapter (Part 2), which will walk you through each step of pizza making, from mixing to baking—and ultimately evaluating and eating your pie! Scan the QR codes throughout the chapter to access instructional videos of techniques. Once you have a handle on those concepts, review the recipes for dough and toppings, selecting a skill level suited to you. Regardless of your pizza making experience, I highly recommend that the first pizzas you bake be simple, tomato-sauce-topped Rossa (page 173) and the classic Margherita (page 174), two ideal pies for judging your progress.

For those who are just getting started with making pizza at home, we start with recipes that call for white flour and commercial yeast until you get your footing, dialing in your dough mixing, fermenting, shaping, and baking techniques using reliable ingredients. Once you have confidence, move on to making and maintaining a starter, making naturally leavened pizza dough with high extraction flour, and managing the intricacies of high temperature ovens. This book guides you through each phase, imparting the precious lessons I have learned over the years about how to ferment dough properly, guarantee structural integrity, and coax maximum performance from toppings. You'll get started on the best possible foot in pursuit of the perfect pie.

TOOLS OF THE TRADE

To get started, you'll need some basic equipment, all of which is available at your local kitchen shop or via online retailers; some things you can even improvise with what you already have. Most of the essentials cost $15 or less, and I have included my preferred sources for some items under Resources (page 253).

The Basics

Metric scale: You absolutely must have this scale, which weighs in grams and kilograms and is used for measuring flour, water, and salt. Volume measures like cups are highly inaccurate so I don't even include them in the dough recipes.

Milligram scale: I highly recommend buying a scale that weighs fractions of a gram for measuring yeast. You can, theoretically, use a level ¼ tablespoon for measuring commercial yeast (it's roughly 1 gram). But it's not 100 percent accurate.

Digital kitchen thermometer: You'll need this for measuring the temperature of your ingredients, which you will plug into the equations for desired dough temperature (page 62) and desired starter temperature (page 62). You can use the digital kitchen thermometer to measure the air temperature as well.

Oven thermometer: Not all oven dials reflect the actual heat of the oven. Use a high heat oven thermometer for accurate readings.

Timer: You'll definitely need a reliable way to keep track of autolyse and resting periods (see page 69), "stretch and fold" intervals, and baking times. You probably have one on your phone already.

Mixing bowls: You'll need large, nonreactive bowls for mixing dough and smaller ones for holding your prepared toppings.

Dough scraper: This is a handy tool for dividing dough, cleaning surfaces, and generally helping move and shape dough.

Kitchen towels: Keep a stack on deck for keeping your hands clean and your surfaces dry.

Pizza peel: I like using a wooden peel (never metal) for launching my pizzas into the oven, but I'll improvise and even use a clean 12-inch piece of rigid cardboard in a pinch.

Baking stone or steel: A stone or steel absorbs and retains heat, which is transferred to the undercarriage of your pizza, allowing for an efficient and successful bake. I highly recommend the Baking Steel created by Andris Lagsdin.

Cooling rack: Land your baked pizzas on a cooling rack to prevent steam from collecting between the counter and undercarriage, which is a recipe for soggy pizza.

Caliper and ruler: Measure the thickness of vegetable and cured meat slices so you can dial in the correct thickness for an even bake every time. If you don't have one, a ruler is a good backup. Use a ruler to measure pizza dimensions when using the Pizza Evaluation Rubric (page xviii).

Square pans: Any black square or rectangular pans can make a great pie. I use 16-inch LloydPans.

If You Want to Invest in Additional Tools

Spiral mixer: I love mixing pizza dough by hand, but at home I occasionally use an Italian-made Famag (Fabbrica Macchine Alimentari Grillo) mixer, available in a number of models and sizes, imported by Pleasant Hill Grain. The series S models with tilting heads and removable bowls are easier to clean than the standard fixed versions.

High temperature ovens: If you can afford to build a wood fired stone hearth oven in your backyard, I recommend California-based Mugnaini and New York–based Forza Forni (the importer of Pavesi ovens). Other high heat outdoor oven brands that are more affordable include Ooni and Gozney. The Breville Pizzaiolo works indoors and fits on a countertop.

Wood moisture meter: Ensure the moisture of the wood for your wood fired oven is as close to 15 percent as possible. They are sold at hardware stores, big box stores, and online.

Fire bricks: Position directly below the stone or steel to provide additional thermal mass (see page 108) to your oven, which shortens recovery time and helps the oven retain heat for successive bakes. They are sold at hardware stores, big box stores, and online.

PART 1

WHERE PIZZA BEGINS

INGREDIENTS AND HOW TO CHOOSE THEM

At Razza, we evaluate every pie against our almost 60-point idea of perfection, but the idea of using rubrics to help make more delicious pizza came earlier. The very first rubrics I created were for ingredients: tomatoes (page 53), extra-virgin olive oil (page 54), and mozzarella (page 55). Collectively I called them the 40 Points, and they are where the journey to extraordinary pizza begins. You might be tempted to skip this section and jump right to the dough recipes: Don't! I take a holistic approach to pizza making and no one element is more important than another.

Every time we taste a new brand of canned tomatoes, oil, or mozzarella, my staff and I analyze it and take copious notes about its characteristics and potential. If this sounds insane, I urge you to stay with me. Pizza making, like bread baking, is a craft. Success is the product of the raw materials you start with, and the techniques you use to transform them. Anyone can make an edible pizza. But going further, mastering each step along the way—beginning with ingredient selection—can create something spectacular. Plus, it's fun to learn more about flour from millers, tomatoes from canners, and mozzarella from cheese makers. In fact, these are the first steps in making the best pizza you've ever had. (They may even be the first steps in making the best *anything* you've ever had.) When you understand your ingredients and how they work together and independently, you become a better cook and baker.

After several years of building on these ingredient rubrics, I realized a critical part of the equation was missing. We needed a set of criteria against which to judge each finished pie. The 40 Points were soon joined by the Pizza Evaluation Rubric.

It might seem out of place to introduce you to the score sheet for a finished pizza before you even mix dough. But analyzing the ingredients and considering how they will impact the finished product is an essential step on the journey to making your perfect pie.

Familiarize yourself with the elements of the Pizza Evaluation Rubric (page xviii) so that as you're considering your flour, yeast, and toppings choices, plus your mixing, fermenting, and shaping techniques, you have a clear handle on what you're aiming to produce. Before you intend to bake, print out a stack of rubrics so you can ensure you're hitting the marks or note where your craft would benefit from improvement.

This chapter will go beyond the 40 Points rubrics for tomatoes, oil, and cheese and will delve deeply into other ingredients like flour and seasonal toppings as well. I have some good news for enthusiastic note takers: A great way to keep track of all these wonderful things as you are discovering your favorite ingredients is to write down feedback as you taste raw ingredients and consider how they will impact the finished product. That way, as you approach your next pizza session, you can improve on what you noted the last time and work toward your ideal pie without having to start from scratch each time. I keep a notebook in my kitchen so I can record dated observations and I highly recommend that you do, too!

While the blueprint I lay out in the following pages maps my approach to great ingredients, I encourage you to make them your own once you master the basics. You can apply this philosophy to any pizza toppings you enjoy—and to cooking in general. Just think about how much your cooking would improve if you applied the 40 Points treatment to the ingredients in chicken soup, grilled cheese, or anything else you love.

DOUGH

Dough forms the base for your pizza and is composed of flour, water, salt, and yeast in the form of either commercial yeast or sourdough starter. The type of flour and yeast you choose, the hydration (see page 66) of the dough, and the way you ferment and handle the dough will determine the structure, flavor, and characteristics of the baked pizza; there are other factors such as bake time and temperature but we will delve into those later. When they are all in harmony, the outcome is my ideal pie. In the pages that follow, I will break down the essential ingredients for making dough, which are critical to understanding how to mix, ferment, handle, and bake the dough recipes in Part 3.

FLOUR

Flour accounts for more weight in your pizza dough than any other ingredient. Accordingly, the type you choose impacts the dough in a big way, and makes the difference between a tough pizza and a tender one. Unlike tomatoes and cheese, which you can assess in their raw state, flour offers no such opportunity—bags of flour even carry warnings against tasting it raw. The best way to judge flour is to bake with it, then reflect on the finished product. I have taken some of the guesswork out of choosing flour for you. But even so, there is quite a bit of variation among

brands and even more so among flours made from different grains. The key to understanding flour is to practice with it. Repetition is essential to cracking the flour code.

As a former student at Cook College, Rutgers University's agriculture school, I believe in supporting domestic farmers, so I reach for American flours when baking. The U.S. is one of the biggest wheat producers in the world and there are some incredibly consistent, widely available, and affordable conventional flours on the market. There is also extremely high quality artisan flour being made from domestic wheat, thanks to hardworking farmers and dedicated millers across the country.

The most basic recipes in the book call for conventional all-purpose or bread flour, while the more advanced recipes use freshly milled flour made from heritage grains sourced from artisan mills. Even in the case of the former, I prefer an industrial American flour to its imported counterparts. I also choose American flour for environmental reasons: It has a smaller carbon footprint than imported flour and buying it promotes the domestic flour market. The more we support American flour, the more it will remain readily available to bakers across the country and the more the industry will continue to improve.

In the conventional flour category, there are several brands sold in all fifty states—King Arthur, Heckers, and Gold Medal among them.

I learned to make pizza using those brands and I suggest you do, too, because they are so standardized, consistent, and accessible. The white flour recipes in this book were developed and tested using King Arthur unbleached all-purpose flour.

Conventional flour is milled to have specific characteristics that don't vary from bag to bag or year to year. As your baking advances, you can move on to whole wheat flour, high extraction flour, and freshly milled flour, all of which have their own variables to manage and require a good handle on dough making to produce the best results. In the past decade, artisan mills have made great strides in providing consistent specs but I'll delve into what makes working with their flours more challenging in other ways in the coming pages.

WHERE DOES FLOUR COME FROM?

Flour is obtained by milling wheat. It all starts in the field, where the wheat plant grows seeds called wheat berries. A wheat berry is composed of bran (the outer shell), endosperm (the carbohydrate-rich material that produces white flour when milled), and germ (the reproductive component of the seed). I relate it to an egg: Bran is the sharp eggshell, the endosperm is the protein-rich egg white, and the germ is the fatty yolk. The bran and germ, otherwise known as the whole wheat components, make up about 15 to 20 percent of the wheat berry's total weight; the remaining 80 to 85 percent is endosperm.

When the wheat berries are harvested, mainly through mechanical means, they pass through a series of steps before they ever see the mill. First, they have their fibrous outer chaff removed, then they are washed and dried to lower their internal humidity, making them ideal for long-term storage without spoiling. The dried kernel is relatively shelf-stable, so as soon as it reaches that ideal moisture it can be milled immediately or stored for later milling.

There are a number of types of mills that wheat berries can pass through in order to become flour. For most of human history, stone milling was used to process grain. It features two stones; one stone is anchored to a base, while the other spins on top

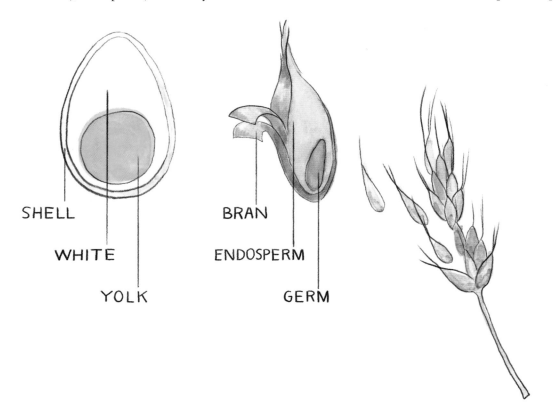

SHELL

WHITE

YOLK

BRAN

ENDOSPERM

GERM

of it. As grains are fed into the space between the stones, they are crushed into whole wheat flour, which includes the bran, germ, and endosperm of the wheat berry. The stone mills operating today may choose to bag the entire mixture to make whole wheat flour, sift out some bran and germ for high extraction flour, or sift out all of it to produce white flour.

Most mills employ the steel roller mill, rotating cylinders used to pulverize grain or other products. Industrial mills sift out the bran and germ, isolating the endosperm to produce white flour. They may also add it back in to make high extraction or whole wheat flour. For well over a century, roller milling has been the standard in flour production as it is the fastest and most efficient way to pulverize wheat and produce industrial flour.

White flour is shelf-stable due to the absence of bran and germ, which have oils and other substances that degrade and go rancid. It is composed of proteins and carbohydrates, and fortified with vitamins and minerals like niacin, riboflavin, thiamine, other B vitamins, and iron. The vast majority of the flour on the market from the late 19th century to today has been white flour, replacing millennia of whole wheat and high extraction flour baking.

In some ways, the advent of commodity flour was a good thing. Flour with a longer shelf life can feed more people. And industrial products can create predictable results. But what is gained in shelf stability and consistency is lost in flavor, nutrition, and complexity. The absence of bran and germ extends the life of white flour but robs it of nutritional value, flavor, and terroir (a sense of place).

CHOOSING THE RIGHT FLOUR

When selecting flour for pizza making, as with all ingredients, I highly recommend working with flour that is consistently available to you. Dough making and pizza baking are a practice. If you work with the same flour over time, you can methodically improve on the quality of your dough because you aren't having to constantly account for new variables and can instead focus on dialing in your process.

It's also important to choose the flour based on your intentions. In my case, I am looking for a flour that, when fermented and baked, produces specific characteristics: an eggshell exterior that is easy to bite through, a tender crumb, and deep crust caramelization. I have found that these attributes are best achieved using relatively lower protein flours (11 to 13 percent) compared to the rest of the pizza industry. Such flours have enough strength to trap gas well, and can be shaped and stretched without tearing, but still yield a tender finished product. (If you wanted a crust that is tough and more difficult to chew through, you would use a higher protein flour.) There are many domestic flour choices, ranging from white flour to whole wheat, that can produce the results I am looking for.

FLOUR CHARACTERISTIC: PROTEIN PERCENTAGE

All wheat flour contains protein, most of which comes from the endosperm; there are also traces of protein in the germ. Since the late 1800s, baking in the U.S. has mainly been done on an industrial scale. Industrial bakers require strong flours (those with high protein content) to stand up to vigorous mechanical mixing and shaping. Accordingly, farmers, millers, and bakers have favored high protein flours, often prioritizing protein content over flavor. Indeed, many pizza makers choose high protein flours weighing in at 14 percent and wrongly believe protein percentage is a mark of flour quality.

When it comes to pizza making, the two most important proteins in endosperm are gliadins and glutenins. When hydrated (when you mix flour with water; see page 66), gliadins and glutenins combine to form gluten, a protein network that traps gases as the dough rises and gives the baked dough its structure. The relative quantities of gliadins and glutenins, along with the hydration of the dough and what point the dough is in its life cycle, are what help to determine where the flour falls on the extensibility/elasticity spectrum. Glutenins are shorter molecules that promote elasticity. Gliadins favor extensibility. For conventional flours, the two tend to be predictably in balance; when you work with single variety grains (see next page), these factors become more evident.

Single Variety Grains

Ancient grains impart flavor, character, and a sense of place to your dough. Some, like emmer and spelt, have been cultivated for thousands of years and have not changed significantly since antiquity. Heritage grains, like Turkey Red and Red Fife, aren't quite as historic. They are grains that were bred prior to the 20th century. Edison and Yecora Rojo are even more modern. Turkey Red and Red Fife are both hard red winter wheats, denoting their pigment and the sowing period; Yecora Rojo is a hard red spring wheat, also alluding to its color and sowing time.

Winter wheat is sown in the fall and harvested in early summer. It may have a slightly lower gluten content than spring wheat but a good balance of glutenin and gliadin and higher protein quality, therefore a higher tolerance to longer fermentation periods. Meanwhile, spring wheat is sown in the spring and harvested in the fall and may have a higher gluten content but lower gluten quality. If you are baking using commercial or heavy mixers and fermenting for a short time, it's great. The characteristics of the flour are ultimately influenced by a range of factors: the farmer, the season, the location, and the farming practices among them.

Hard wheats tend to have higher gluten content so they are generally used for breads, pasta, and pizza, while soft wheat has lower gluten content so it makes more tender products like cakes and pastries. It's not a given that your all-purpose or bread flour mix contains only milled hard wheat. There may be some soft wheat in the mix, albeit a small percentage.

When buying flour, the type of wheat (hard vs. soft, winter vs. spring) may not be indicated on the label, so the best way to get this and other information is to build a relationship with the miller and ask tons of questions. Some of the most gratifying and joyous moments of my baking career have been spent just chatting with a miller about his or her flour types.

Generally speaking, ancient grains were snubbed for the bulk of the 20th century by the commodity flour industry, which was more interested in high protein and high yield grains. But these historic crops have survived thanks to small scale farmers and millers, and in the past quarter century have seen a resurgence as artisan bakers look to them to provide unparalleled flavor and nutrition.

You can use any single variety grain you wish for recipes like "Choose Your Own Adventure" Dough (page 163) as long as its protein quality (see next page) is high and the protein percentage ranges from 11 to 13 percent. For industrial flours, I recommend 11 to 13 percent throughout the book, but some grains like Edison have lower protein but still make fantastic pizza. Look for them online or at your local mill. Or even better, take this as an opportunity to call or visit a mill, speak to the miller about your pizza making, and learn to use the grains she or he is milling.

The subject of ancient, heritage, and modern grains could be a book in its own right but here are some of the ones I love to use:

GRAIN	ANCIENT/ HERITAGE/ MODERN	TYPE
Edison	Modern	Hard white wheat
Emmer	Ancient	
Red Fife	Heritage	Hard red winter wheat
Spelt	Ancient	
Turkey Red	Heritage	Hard red winter wheat
Yecora Rojo	Modern	Hard red spring wheat

Elasticity in dough means that it will spring back to its original shape when stretched, somewhat like a rubber band. You can also observe elasticity when you're shaping a pizza and the dough contracts or when the dough rises as gases are trapped during fermentation. Extensibility refers to the capacity of a dough to be stretched without tearing or snapping back. It is analogous to stretching out a cheap cotton shirt that doesn't snap back to its original shape. To see a dough's extensibility in action, lift it with one hand and allow the dough to sag. An extensible dough will stretch out easily and not return to its shape. A good balance of elasticity and extensibility is ideal for pizza dough, which should trap a lot of gas as the dough rises and hold together when you stretch the dough before baking.

While it is certainly important to know a flour's protein percentage, this figure is not the be all and end all. It's much more important to understand how the flour's glutenin and gliadin interact with one another and what the outcome of a low protein or high protein flour dough is. This is ascertained by mixing, fermenting, and baking.

FLOUR CHARACTERISTIC: PROTEIN QUALITY

Protein quality is related to the ability of the flour to hold up and not break down under force (kneading) or long fermentation (the gluten structure breaks down over time as the dough ferments) and is an indicator of whether the wheat was grown properly and harvested at the correct time. If you're fermenting your dough for a short time, protein quality isn't as important. For longer fermentation times, including for the recipes in this book, it is much more of a factor. Even "strong" dough made from flour with a high protein percentage could have poor protein quality and break down during the dough making process.

Protein percentage is simple to quantify, but protein quality is a more complicated factor. Determining protein quality in advance of using a flour is difficult unless you have a product spec sheet (and even if you have one, it practically takes a degree in chemistry to decipher it all). Realistically, it's just a case of working with the flour to see how it behaves during long fermentation periods. If it stands up to a long fermentation without deteriorating (tearing when you stretch the dough, for example) and has a long window in which the dough is at its prime (at the ideal maturity for stretching and baking), the protein quality is high. I find that generally, commercial flour brands like King Arthur have sufficient protein quality to make a great product.

FLOUR CHARACTERISTIC: ASH CONTENT

Ash content refers to a flour's mineral content. To quantify this, a portion of flour is burned in a lab and the charred minerals left behind are weighed. Most minerals in wheat are present in the bran and germ, so the amount of ash correlates to how much of them are in the flour. Emulating French flour nomenclature, some American mills use the ash figure to name their flours. For example, T85 flour has 0.85 percent ash, an indication that the flour is high extraction flour containing a high proportion of both bran and germ. T70, by contrast, is lower. The higher the ash content number, the greater flavor potential and nutritional value the flour has thanks to the higher proportion of bran and germ. Higher ash content also makes the flour more challenging to work with due to the presence of bran, which "cuts" gluten strands and inhibits gluten development.

BAKING WITH COMMODITY FLOUR

The average bag of white flour from your local supermarket is a standardized industrial product that has been subjected to intensive testing in order to fulfill the desired specs of the mill (protein percentage, for example). It's rare that a bag will list the type and provenance of the wheat (a single bag may contain a blend of wheat obtained from crops grown in Canada or the United States).

White flour lacks the flavor and nutrition of its whole wheat counterpart. So why use it? I believe it's important to learn to crawl before you walk. Use something consistent and reliable until you understand fermentation and isolate all the other variables involved in baking and pizza making, like time and temperature. Until you understand all the variables individually you can't control them

(Continued on page 12)

Flour Terminology

Walk down the baking aisle of any supermarket and you'll encounter at least a dozen types of flour. There isn't a whole lot of explicit information on labels and often you're given the bare minimum (type, protein percentage, nutritional information, and suggested use). There's also no standard nomenclature for imported flour, and France and Italy both have their own unique labeling customs and ways of describing flour. The world of flour labeling and marketing is a wild one, so it's important to know what (and what not!) to look for when shopping (recommended types are starred *).

*All-purpose flour	White flour formulated to have a medium protein percentage (10 to 12 percent) so it can be used for either pastries (which require a low percentage of protein) or breads (which require a higher percentage).
Bleached flour	Flour that has been made with a bleaching agent that removes its natural pigmentation. It is ideal for making squishy white bread or noodles but I don't recommend it for pizza.
*Bread flour	May be white or whole wheat. It has a protein percentage that ranges from 12 to 14 percent.
Bromated flour	Flour that has been treated with potassium bromate (a banned substance in many countries) to improve flour's elasticity potential and to give it greater rising and oven spring potential. I never use bromated flour.
*Enriched flour	White flour that has had vitamins and minerals added to it to replace the nutritional value it lost when the bran and germ were sifted out. Most commodity flours are enriched.
*High extraction flour	Any flour that has had a portion of the bran and germ sifted out. High extraction flour may also be called bolted flour.
Pizza flour	Marketed as being formulated with pizza making in mind. There is no standardization between mills, so you don't know how the flour will behave until you bake with it. I like control over my dough and believe "pizza flour" is a marketing ploy that can't be trusted so I avoid it altogether.
*T85	High extraction flour with 0.85 percent ash content, so it has a nice mineral composition. Many artisan mills label their flour with a numerical figure related to ash content.
*Whole grain flour	A broad term including whole wheat, as well as the entire milled seed of other grains like rye and spelt.
*Whole wheat flour	Flour containing the entire milled wheat berry: endosperm, bran, and germ. It is also called 100 percent inclusion flour.
"00" flour	Finely milled white flour in Italy. A mill may have a number of "00" flours, each designed for different uses based on protein percentage.

The Myth of Italian "00" Flour

A lot of bakers select their flour based on marketing alone; there is a particularly strong narrative in the pizza world that finely milled "00" ("doppio zero" or "double zero") Italian flour is best for pizza. That is not altogether true. The "00" simply means a highly processed, very powdery flour in Italian baking terms. It can be made from soft wheat, creating a tender dough ideal for cookies, or from hard wheat, ideal for pasta, or a blend of the two, which can be used for bread and pizza.

The popularity of "00" flour in pizza making is mainly due to aggressive marketing by flour brands and the fact that it is the milling fineness of choice for Neapolitan pizzaioli. In Naples, it makes sense to use locally milled Italian "00" flour—it's what's traditional and available, though it should be noted that lots of Italian flour is actually made from commodity wheat grown in North America and Eastern Europe and shipped in for milling. By the time this "Italian flour" reaches American shores, it's been on quite a journey—in some cases from North America in wheat berry form, to Italy, then back again. There are plenty of domestic American flours adapted to pizza making—look for anything with a protein content of 11 to 13 percent, including some all-purpose flours and high extraction flours. Please do not use "00" flour for the recipes in this book.

collectively. White flour takes out some of the guesswork.

Even with white flour—as devoid of character, sense of place, and natural elements of the wheat as it is—you can still coax great flavors out of it through fermentation: By fermenting the dough slowly, the yeast produces alcohol and organic acids that are flavor compounds. Look at white flour as a blank canvas for painting the flavors of fermentation upon.

BAKING WITH WHOLE WHEAT FLOUR

When making pizza dough, I never use 100 percent whole wheat flour. The bran and the germ affect gluten development (think of the bran shards like little razors slicing through it) and therefore don't create the airy crumb (interior structure) that I love.

You *can* make great pizza using a portion of whole wheat flour, but I recommend using it in one of two ways. The first is to incorporate it by using sourdough starter made with whole wheat. In the sourdough recipes that follow, all of the whole wheat is contributed by the starter. Another way is to blend it with white flour for yeasted dough. In both cases, it does take some practice to get great results. If you don't have experience baking with whole wheat and want to use whole wheat flour alongside white flour, blend it in incrementally. Start with 5 percent of the total flour weight, then work up to 20 percent as you gain confidence with this new material.

BAKING WITH FRESHLY MILLED LOCAL FLOUR

Regions like New England, the Carolinas, upstate New York, and the Pacific Northwest are at the forefront of the burgeoning local milling movement, but there are also little pockets all over the U.S. where artisan millers are thriving. All across the country, you can find freshly milled flour made from single variety grains that can contribute to amazing flavor and complexity in your dough. If you're lucky enough to live near an artisan mill, the odds are the grain was grown nearby. I love meeting grain farmers through my miller friends and I highly recommend connecting with them, too. In the summer, it never hurts to ask for an invite to the grain harvest, during which the grain is cut down, cleaned, and processed before the wheat berries are prepared for storage. Seriously—try it. Following each step from the field to the mill gives you a great appreciation for how much work goes into each bag of flour.

> Store whole wheat, high extraction, or freshly milled flour in a sealed container in the refrigerator or freezer.

Why I Don't Bake with High Gluten Flour

Bakers should be cautious about being all in on gluten. As mentioned above, American commodity agriculture and baking have historically favored high protein (and therefore high gluten) flours. For this reason, high protein flours have dominated the market for over a century. While high protein flours have their place—think big factories churning out bread that is kneaded intensely to build strength rather than letting it develop slowly through periodic stretch and folds—I reach for slightly lower protein flour, and not just because it gets me the results I'm looking for in my pizza. It's also easier for the human stomach to process.

Gluten, the protein network that is created when you mix flour and water, is an essential element of the baking process, as it provides the structure for trapping gas within it during fermentation. It's something that seems simple enough to grasp if you look at bubbles forming in the dough. The gluten network enables the dough to stretch like a balloon. If that's your only experience with observing gluten, that might give you the idea that it's a delicate substance. In reality, gluten is incredibly tough.

The easiest way to conceptualize gluten is to let a piece of fully developed dough sit under running water for 10 minutes. The water rinses out the starch and isolates the gluten, leaving a tough, rubber-band-like substance behind. Unlike starch, gluten protein isn't water soluble, so its rubbery structure has staying power in your sink—not to mention your gut!

One of the benefits of eating products made with whole wheat is that the bran in them slices the gluten, making it easier to digest. Lower protein flours have a similar effect. Pizza made with lower protein flour is more tender. Your teeth literally have to do less work when biting through the crust than with pizza made with higher protein flour. If the dough was fermented and handled properly, the exterior should shatter, there should be no tugging or gnawing, just lightness and airiness.

The consistency of locally milled grains can vary, though there have been some amazing advances in bag standardization in the past few years. Still, working with locally milled grains remains one of the more challenging arenas for bakers accustomed to conventional flour—it means you have to be intuitive, not rely on a specific hydration percentage, use your senses to determine when the dough is properly hydrated, be able to pivot and really watch your dough, and be in tune with the feel and anticipate how it's going to react hours or days later as it ferments. It's still a great choice if you can source locally milled flour from your farmers' market, local mill, or the internet, especially if you want to support your local food system and agriculture. Just treat it like whole wheat, working in 5 percent by weight to start, and incrementally adding more as you gain confidence.

If you use a locally milled high extraction or whole wheat flour you're going to need a bit more water by weight than you would with a white flour due to the presence of the absorbent bran and germ. You'll see this reflected in the hydration range in the "Choose Your Own Adventure" Dough (page 163). Also, thanks to the nutritional value of bran and germ and the freshness of the flour, the yeast will have more to feed on so the dough will likely ferment faster.

When baking with locally milled flour, follow visual cues for when your dough is ready, rather than the timing referred to in the recipes later in the book. Visual indicators will give you a more accurate and attuned way to determine when your dough is ready. As I like to say when it comes to working with artisan flour: Watch the dough, not the clock!

BAKING WITH HOME MILLED FLOUR

I have a small tabletop mill at home, though it doesn't get much of a workout. It's a fun way to get to know grains and to learn how to harness the energy of very freshly milled flour. But I'm not milling on a commercial scale because it's very difficult to get an excellent, consistent flour (and

FERMENTATION WITH COMMERCIAL YEAST

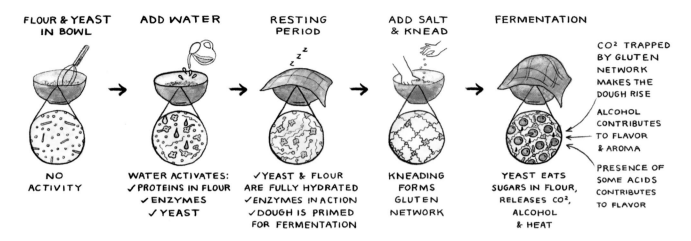

FLOUR & YEAST IN BOWL

NO ACTIVITY

ADD WATER

WATER ACTIVATES:
✓ PROTEINS IN FLOUR
✓ ENZYMES
✓ YEAST

RESTING PERIOD

✓ YEAST & FLOUR ARE FULLY HYDRATED
✓ ENZYMES IN ACTION
✓ DOUGH IS PRIMED FOR FERMENTATION

ADD SALT & KNEAD

KNEADING FORMS GLUTEN NETWORK

FERMENTATION

YEAST EATS SUGARS IN FLOUR, RELEASES CO², ALCOHOL & HEAT

CO_2 TRAPPED BY GLUTEN NETWORK MAKES THE DOUGH RISE

ALCOHOL CONTRIBUTES TO FLAVOR & AROMA

PRESENCE OF SOME ACIDS CONTRIBUTES TO FLAVOR

therefore pizza) without serious milling experience. Plus, I can only mill about 3 kilos of flour per hour.

One concept I have embraced at Razza is that we are part of a community of food makers. We are not farmers and we are not millers, so we entrust experts in those fields with growing grain and milling flour for us—not to mention analyzing the flour for specs and safety. After a few experiments with mediocre home milling results, I learned an important lesson: Just because something is homemade doesn't mean it's great.

If you do want to incorporate home milled grains into your dough, start at 5 percent, working up to 20 percent. The more freshly milled flour you use, the more water you'll need and the faster the dough will ferment thanks to its bran and germ content, which gives the yeast a richer source of food to feast on. Feel free to sift out some of the bran and germ, though be warned it is a messy process. I also recommend monitoring the dough more than you would when using conventional flour as you observe visual cues for readiness.

WATER

If you follow pizza competitions, you're probably wondering why I don't include water as an essential dough ingredient. Famously, pizza makers from New York and Naples travel with their local water so they can mix dough with it at the competition site, as though this liquid has some magical feature that makes their pizza special.

This makes for great mythology, but the truth is that the type of water you use to make dough is irrelevant. If I can make a delicious pizza with the brackish tap water in South Florida, you can use any water of potable quality to make yours. I don't expect Italians to stop flying Neapolitan tap water to the Pizza Expo in Vegas anytime soon, but if they did, there would be more room in their suitcases for the ingredients that really matter in their process, like flour and tomato sauce.

The Hydration box on page 66 breaks down what water does in the pizza making process.

COMMERCIAL YEAST AND PREFERMENTS

Yeast is the engine that drives fermentation in bread and pizza making. There are a number of different types of yeast. The recipes in this book call for either commercial yeast (specifically instant yeast that comes in a packet or container) or sourdough starter (a diverse colony of wild yeast and bacteria that you cultivate from the environment). In both cases, the yeast ferments the dough, transforming the sugars in the flour into byproducts like carbon dioxide, which is trapped

FERMENTATION WITH STARTER

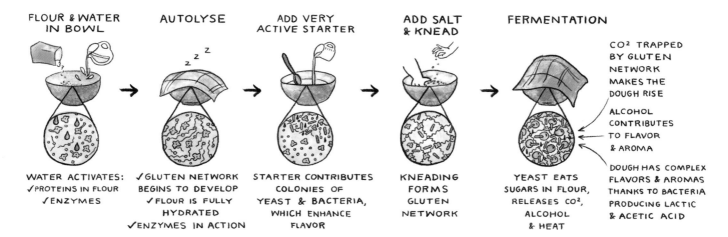

FLOUR & WATER IN BOWL	AUTOLYSE	ADD VERY ACTIVE STARTER	ADD SALT & KNEAD	FERMENTATION
WATER ACTIVATES: ✓PROTEINS IN FLOUR ✓ENZYMES	✓GLUTEN NETWORK BEGINS TO DEVELOP ✓FLOUR IS FULLY HYDRATED ✓ENZYMES IN ACTION	STARTER CONTRIBUTES COLONIES OF YEAST & BACTERIA, WHICH ENHANCE FLAVOR	KNEADING FORMS GLUTEN NETWORK	YEAST EATS SUGARS IN FLOUR, RELEASES CO_2, ALCOHOL & HEAT

On the FERMENTATION step:
- CO_2 TRAPPED BY GLUTEN NETWORK MAKES THE DOUGH RISE
- ALCOHOL CONTRIBUTES TO FLAVOR & AROMA
- DOUGH HAS COMPLEX FLAVORS & AROMAS THANKS TO BACTERIA PRODUCING LACTIC & ACETIC ACID

within the gluten matrix, causing it to expand and making the dough rise.

For a beginner baker, working with commercial yeast yields more consistent results and allows you to practice your craft as you learn the basics of fermentation. With more experience, you can introduce sourdough starter into your baking, which has a steeper learning curve, but can also be part of a joyful lifelong journey of artisan baking.

COMMERCIAL YEAST

All commercial yeast is *Saccharomyces cerevisiae,* a single celled organism that is a really prolific gas producer by nature when it has flour to feed on and water for activity. It comes in several forms: instant yeast, active dry yeast, and fresh (cake) yeast. These three types are really similar, but the moisture content and activation approach differ. I use instant yeast in my yeasted doughs because it doesn't need to be activated (proofed) before mixing so it's just easier to use. It's also easier for most home bakers to track down than fresh yeast. If you wish to use active dry yeast in one of the recipes later in this book, multiply the quantity of instant yeast listed in the ingredients by 1.25 to determine how much active dry yeast you will need. Multiply the instant dry yeast by 3 to determine how much fresh yeast the recipe requires.

PREFERMENTS

A preferment denotes a mixture, typically of flour, water, and yeast, that is fermented independently, then added to bread or pizza dough to act as the leavening agent or for the addition of flavor. Preferments may take the place of commercial yeast in a recipe. They are wonderful because they deliver the benefits of extended fermentation without the risk of gluten breakdown, since you're only pre-fermenting a portion of the total flour weight. The process essentially splits the dough's fermentation into two parts. Preferments contribute serious flavor, greater complexity, improved texture, and a longer shelf life (this last part is more relevant to bread than to pizza, as pizza is generally consumed immediately!). Think of preferments as the stock you add to soup, providing a concentrated impact that improves the overall flavor of your soup.

My preferment of choice is sourdough starter (also called levain, starter, and natural leaven), specifically a 100 percent hydration starter composed of equal parts flour and water. It has a batter-like consistency and is composed of a symbiotic community of yeasts and bacteria; the precise types of yeasts and bacteria depend on the flour and the environment. Preferments can also be made with commercial yeast.

Although the yeast in starter may be a different strain than commercial yeast (and in fact can be several strains, depending on the starter), it acts the same way when fermenting the dough, causing it to rise. Dough made with starter is more flavorful and complex than dough made with commercial yeast because of starter's more complex yeast and bacteria colonies and the coexistence of multiple strains of yeast and bacteria in it. The Fermentation section in Part 2 (page 80) goes a bit deeper into the science of all this and provides a recipe for making and maintaining your own starter.

SALT

When it comes to pizza dough, salt slows down fermentation, strengthens the dough, and is an essential ingredient for flavor. A good, professional bread or pizza dough recipe calls for 2 to 2.5 percent salt by weight with respect to the flour quantity. Anything higher will taste too salty and slow the dough's fermentation too much, and anything less will cause the dough to taste underseasoned. I tend to stay around 2 percent salt because it is adequate for seasoning the dough while not dominating the wheat flavor.

SALT IN THE DOUGH

I use salt in three separate phases of pizza making. The first is in the dough itself. I add it after the flour, water, and leavening agent have been incorporated, scissor pinching it in until it is evenly distributed. I am partial to sea salt, which is often still harvested in traditional ways—channeling seawater into pools to slowly evaporate the water with sunlight and wind. The result is a naturally produced salt that pays homage to millennia-old practices and supports small local communities. I use fine sea salt for dough because its tiny particles are easier to evenly disperse and dissolve than larger ones. Use natural sea salt, which is sold at supermarkets everywhere, and avoid any salt that has additives.

SALT FOR THE TOPPINGS AND CONDIMENTS

I use fine sea salt to season tomato sauce (page 243) so it dissolves quickly; my sauce is uncooked, but more on that later. For all other pizza toppings and condiments, you can use any type of salt, as long as it's not produced with an anti-caking agent. When I use salt for some toppings and condiments like Roasted Mushrooms (page 185) and Fermented Chili Sauce (page 248), I add salt by weight per the Cook's Percentages concept (see page 185). In other words, salt is listed by weight in relation to the main ingredient (mushrooms or chilis, for example). Applying a salt percentage for such recipes guarantees accuracy and consistency from one batch to the next.

Salt is also essential for preparing certain ingredients. Salting zucchini in advance, for example, draws out some of its moisture and changes its texture, ensuring it cooks more evenly and has a pleasant final texture. Just as salt slows and controls fermentation in dough, it also has a similar effect on other organic materials, which is why it is a key ingredient to controlling fermentation in Fermented Chili Sauce.

SALT FOR POST-BAKE SEASONING

Before or after the bake, I use coarse sea salt to provide a pop of salinity. This is where I really geek out on sea salt from all over the world. There are so many unique and individual salts that have a sense of terroir. Depending on my mood, I may use wonderful, slightly damp mineral-rich salt from Northern France, Persian salt with its surreal blue specks, or fine powdery salt from Japan. That said, the salt you choose won't have a massive impact on the final flavor of your toppings. I don't have a strict rubric or guidelines guiding my choice; it's more about incorporating a special salt that I like. Don't use specialty salt in mixing dough or cooking toppings.

TOPPINGS

The universe of toppings encompasses a huge range of ingredients and, by extension, flavors and characteristics. Whenever I am topping a pizza, I contemplate what an ingredient tastes like on its own, how it would interact with the other ingredients, and how it would weigh down or inhibit the structural integrity of the pizza. I also take into consideration the ideal size for eating well and being able to navigate in a single bite. Consider the approach of a sushi chef who tailors each piece to the size of a diner's mouth versus a pizzaiolo who tops a pie with onion rounds that slap you in the chin due to their unwieldy size.

There's also a huge opportunity to create joy with your topping selections. Connecting with a great farmer or produce purveyor, butcher, or cheese maker will absolutely transform the pizza eating experience by drawing you even closer to the products from which it is made. I lay out pizza recipes in Part 4, but I also love freestyling with kitchen leftovers or choosing new combinations based on travel inspiration. I find infinite joy in choosing toppings driven by all sorts of avenues—creativity, necessity, and availability.

UNCOOKED TOMATO SAUCE

Tomatoes aren't just an essential part of the sauce for my pizzas, they are the *only* ingredient aside from a small amount of salt. While some pizza makers add garlic, pepper, oregano, or basil to their sauce, I only use crushed or milled whole canned tomatoes (or milled fresh tomatoes in season). They provide sweetness, moisture, savoriness, and an acidic counterpoint that cuts through the fattiness of cheese; in the case of the Rossa (page 173), the tomatoes stand out on their own, showcasing their glorious flavor spectrum.

In order to preserve the brightness and acidity of the tomatoes, I never cook my sauce before it goes on the raw dough. Instead, I let all the cooking happen while the pizza is baking. For a successful bake, the temperature of the oven, the bake time, and the moisture of the tomatoes must be in sync so they lose just enough moisture to slightly reduce, resulting in a sauce that is not too wet for the dough and toppings and is cooked ever so slightly to concentrate its flavors without over-reducing the liquid and becoming overly acidic and pasty. A sauce that is too cooked will be thick with an over-concentrated flavor. A sauce that is too watery will make the pizza soggy, causing the tip to sag, the crust to underbake, and the toppings to slide off.

CANNED TOMATOES

Tomatoes originated in Mesoamerica, where they were eaten for millennia, but were only introduced to Italy in the 16th century. Due to their low caloric value, as well as superstitious affiliation with poison and eroticism, they weren't adopted into Italian cuisine until the 18th century after their negative associations had worn off. As they gained popularity, their commercial value was extended through canning, which can preserve tomatoes for a year or more. The steps of the canning process haven't changed much over the years: The fruit is harvested, blanched to remove its skin, then transferred to a can and covered with tomato puree. The can is then sealed and subjected to heat to pasteurize it, preserving its contents.

What has changed is selective breeding that enables farmers to grow tomatoes that ripen on the vine all at once, have a thicker skin to reduce damage during transport, and resist pests and blight. In the past, these changes in the service of yield and durability didn't always accompany improved flavor. Today, tomato growers are often just as interested in how a tomato tastes as in how it travels. The technology continues at the cannery, where traditional hand sorting has been replaced with high-tech mechanical sorters that eliminate blemished or damaged fruit.

Every producer uses a proprietary approach for processing their tomatoes. Some treat the blanched tomatoes with a firming agent such as calcium chloride to toughen the flesh for transport. Others cook and concentrate the puree the tomatoes are packed in, while some merely strain out the seeds and preserve the juice's natural viscosity. The variation makes testing multiple canned tomatoes side by side an essential step to determining which one you want to use on your pizza, as well as honing your palate to identify quality (or lack thereof).

TASTING TOMATOES

My ideal canned tomato is bright red in color with a perfect balance of sweetness and acidity and the original and pure tomato flavor intact. This concept seems simple, but climate, season, soil, variety, harvesting methods, and the canning process are all variables that influence every aspect of the whole peeled tomato you use—and therefore the tomato sauce. This section will teach you how to taste tomatoes and break down the essential components for the tomato's ideal texture, color, viscosity, seed to flesh ratio, flavor, acidity, and sweetness.

The Tomato Evaluation Rubric (page 53) was one of the first I wrote when the 40 Points were just a loose set of criteria. It helped me identify and put into words what I didn't like—the thick, pasty, acidic, over-reduced sauce found in many pizzerias across the country—and began to shape what I did like—a balanced flavor of sweetness and acidity, a velvety texture, the correct moisture balance, and a fresh tomato flavor. Verbalizing my preferences with a rubric is how I learned that when it comes to tomatoes, you want to do as little as possible to them after finding the canned tomato you like best, only gently cajoling it into its role.

When choosing canned tomatoes regularly throughout the year, I conduct a raw taste test of numerous brands side by side to determine their relative quality and identify their positive and negative attributes, and I always avoid tomatoes with added ingredients like sugar and herbs. Raw tastings are an easy way to eliminate low quality tomatoes; if they don't taste good in their raw state, they won't taste good cooked. It's apparent when you are tasting a poor quality tomato next to a great one. Taste any run-of-the-mill brand like Muir Glen next to a premium brand like Gustarosso, for example, and the negative flavor attributes of the former will be even more obvious when contrasted with the glorious flavors of the latter. It's also helpful to taste with at least one other person so you can really talk about what you're tasting and compare notes. You can learn a lot listening to someone else evaluate a tomato.

These steps are for assessing the quality of tomatoes. Choose the best brand based on the rubric and prepare the sauce according to the tomato sauce recipes on page 243.

Step 1: Open the can. Transfer the whole tomatoes and their puree to a white bowl.

Step 2: Inspect them for blemishes, fungus or disease, areas of under-ripeness (yellow or green parts), and any bits of remaining skin. Don't dismiss the product if there are some under-ripe bits. Tomatoes are the product of agriculture, after all, so there are bound to be some inconsistencies. But you do want the fruit to be ripe and in good condition. Note if the tomatoes appear soft or firm.

> **Note the color.** Ideally, the tomatoes should be a bright, vibrant, and red-ripe color. Any brownish tint suggests the tomato has oxidized or has a defect caused by canning done at extreme temperatures. A lackluster yellow or pink may signify the tomatoes were under-ripe when harvested.

Step 3: Break open a tomato with a fork. Feel the flesh with your fingers and note its firmness or softness. Pick off any remaining skin, which will affect the sauce's mouthfeel. If you see skins or under-ripe bits, remove and discard them. Observe the prevalence of seeds. I aim for the smallest amount of seeds due to their unappealing texture. Crush the tomatoes by hand or in a food mill.

Step 4: Use a spoon to taste the tomato sauce.

> **Negative flavor attributes:** When I'm tasting, the first things I look for are negative flavor attributes. Do the tomatoes taste "off" or metallic? If so, those flavors will come across in the cooked pizza. Canneries have control over the temperature at which they cook the tomatoes and that has a big influence on what the tomato tastes like. The ones cooked at a higher temperature may have a cooked flavor and dull taste.

> **Positive flavor attributes:** Next, I isolate positive flavor attributes. I want clean and pure flavors that taste close to that of an actual fresh, ripe tomato. In reality, no sauce will ever taste exactly like that because it has been heated during the canning process. But when they're close, that is thanks to the lower temperature cooking method, which gently preserves the freshness and color of

the tomato. Some widely available brands that use this method are Bianco DiNapoli and Gustarosso.

Assess acidity and sweetness: I assess these two categories together because I am interested in them individually, as well as their relationship to one another. You could quantify the strength of acidity with a pH meter and sweetness with a refractometer, which measures the Brix (sweetness index) of the tomato. But I find the best judge of acidity and sweetness and their relation to one another is your taste buds. I reached this conclusion after rigorously testing acidity and sweetness levels with scientific instruments and comparing how my ideal tomato tasted versus others that did not have the textbook perfect measurements but tasted amazing nevertheless.

Acidity: I look for a bright and lively tomato flavor. The pH of canned tomatoes must be 4.6 or lower, based on food safety requirements to prevent botulism from growing in the can. If the tomatoes don't provide this naturally, canners will add citric acid to lower the pH to a food safe level. The pH, however, doesn't always align with the acidity your tongue perceives because pH indicates the strength of the acidity and not the actual quantity of the acidity.

The acidity should be evident but balanced. You should reflexively salivate in response to the acidity. While tasting for acidity, you are trying to predict whether it will cut through guanciale or cheese on the finished product. Ask yourself, *Will I get heartburn after eating it?* A tomato that is too acidic may give you indigestion.

Sweetness: Look for balanced sweetness. The sauce should not taste like sugar or artificial sweetener but rather should be sweet like ripe fruit. Some canned tomato products are cloyingly sweet and that may be because either they lack acidity or contain added sugar or high fructose corn syrup. The latter is common in prepared (jarred) tomato and pizza sauces (see opposite page), which is one of the many reasons I avoid them altogether.

Assess salinity: Tomatoes are naturally savory but canners may add salt to their whole peeled tomatoes. Taste the sauce and assess whether it needs additional salt. It should taste seasoned but not salty. Just as I did with the pH meter and refractometer, I bought a salinometer to test the salt content of a range of tomato brands. The actual salt level did not always match up with what I perceived as the salt level in each sample. The salinometer is collecting dust next to the other testing instruments on a shelf in the restaurant. Once again, the most important tools you have are your own taste buds and intuition. If, based on your assessment, the tomatoes need seasoning, add fine sea salt a pinch at a time, stirring to completely dissolve. Taste and add more salt a pinch at a time as needed until you hit your desired seasoning level.

Mouthfeel: We have already evaluated the tomato's texture visually in Step 2 above. The tactile analysis of a tomato's texture is called mouthfeel. As the word implies, it is all about what the tomato sauce feels like on your palate. It should coat the mouth and be velvety and luscious, never watery.

There is a successive mouthfeel assessment as part of the Tomato Evaluation Rubric (page 53) once the tomato has been cooked on the pizza. When I evaluate cooked tomato for mouthfeel, I use the Rossa (page 173) as the benchmark because its main topping is tomato sauce.

Viscosity: You can measure viscosity (thickness) with a Bostwick Consistometer, but you don't need a $400 instrument if you practice tasting and observation. Viscosity is determined by the amount of tomato solids in the sauce and how they flow. It is one of those major factors that a pizza maker needs to take into account before putting sauce on the pizza. It impacts how fast or slow the liquid in the sauce will evaporate and reduce in the oven and how the sauce will flow and interact with the toppings. When analyzing the tomato sauce for viscosity, note how thick or loose the sauce is. You want actual tomato solids and pulp in a juicy liquid, but you don't want the sauce to be too loose or too thick—otherwise the tomato won't cook properly and the sauce will be too wet or over-reduced.

When you are making your first pizzas, assess how the viscosity of the raw sauce translates to the finished product. A sauce cooked in a home oven at 500°F for 6 to 7 minutes may reduce differently than the same sauce cooked in a high temperature oven for a shorter bake. The consistency of the tomatoes can be adjusted after you bake the first pizza—I call this the Test Pie (see page 171). Add a bit of water to sauce that reduces heavily in the oven and strain sauce that remains damp on the crust (it's rare for canned tomato sauce to be too thin; this is more of a consideration with sauce made from fresh seasonal tomatoes). There are other ways to impact the cooked tomato viscosity: You can put less sauce on the pizza, or put the sauce on top of the cheese instead of underneath it. You can also alternate dollops of sauce and cheese, as on the Jersey Margherita (page 177).

Pizza Sauce

I don't even consider using jarred flavored tomato sauces or premade "pizza sauce." I am only interested in cooking with quality whole peeled canned tomatoes or fresh tomatoes in season. No manufacturer is going to use high quality tomatoes in their prepared sauces because they are obscenely expensive. Most just don't use high quality anything, from the produce to the olive oil to the herbs, and they often employ an arsenal of seasonings to mask "off" flavors.

Cooked Sauces

Though the rubric is really aimed at assessing whole canned tomatoes, a cooked tomato sauce can have a place on a pizza. I don't typically make a cooked tomato sauce purposefully for putting on pizza (it challenges the whole texture, acidity, and viscosity argument laid out here). But if I do have leftover cooked tomato sauce in my refrigerator and I'm out of whole canned tomatoes, I will use it. But I dilute the cooked sauce a bit with water, since it will have been concentrated through cooking and will lose even more moisture during the bake. Consider the sauce's sweetness and acidity and imagine what it will taste like cooked, then choose toppings to complement.

OLIVE OIL

Depending on when it's used, olive oil may contribute flavor (a small amount if added before the bake, and a greater amount after), contribute fat (always), or transfer heat to the toppings (during the bake). I nearly always drizzle olive oil over raw toppings, but consider the fat content of those toppings before adding additional oil to the finished product. Use any quality extra-virgin olive oil you like that passes the taste test outlined in the pages that follow, paired with the Olive Oil Evaluation Rubric (page 54). But if you have a choice of different oils, reflect on how they might work best on a pizza. An oil with very assertive notes would stand up to toppings with strong flavors. An oil that is very delicate will get lost.

I was at an extra-virgin olive oil producer in California recently and our guide summed up this ingredient simply and elegantly: extra-virgin olive oil is juice. To put it more decadently, extra-virgin olive oil is the fatty juice of fresh olives. It can be made in a number of ways. Artisan producers harvest the olives, then pulverize the fruit with stone or steel. In artisanal production, the paste is pressed or passed through a centrifuge to separate the fresh green oil from the olive solids. The final product, extra-virgin olive oil, is then bottled and sold. Larger producers may use expeller presses (also known as screw presses) or heat and chemicals to extract the oil.

The recipes in this book call for extra-virgin olive oil only. There are many grades of olive oil on the market but only extra-virgin can be of quality. That's not to say all extra-virgin olive oil is good, hence the need to taste test. But I can assure you olive oil that is not extra-virgin is subpar commodity oil and does not have the flavor, pungency, or clean finish I insist on for my pizzas.

We use extra-virgin olive oil on many of our pizzas, some before the bake, some before *and* after. There are a few pizzas, like Guancia (page 203) and Pepperoni (page 200) that we do not drizzle with any oil; they have enough fat coming from their toppings. Use similar discretion when creating your own pies.

We always have a half dozen olive oils on rotation at the restaurant and at home, ranging from affordable and delicious to exceptional and outrageously expensive. We save the really fancy stuff for drizzling on salads, seafood, steaks, and cooked pizza. We use the affordable (but still high quality) oil on pizzas before the bake. It will cook in the oven, and therefore lose some of its aromatic, nutritional, and flavor compounds. Delicious, nuanced olive oil is so delicate we don't want to subject it to the high heat of the oven. If you don't have an arsenal of oils, you can use the same extra-virgin olive oil before and after the bake as long as it's high quality. We don't have a favorite brand per se, but we generally stick to domestic oils that are certified by the California Olive Oil Council (COOC) or Olive Oil Commission of California (OOCC) and labeled accordingly, indicating the oils adhere to rigorous quality standards. However, neither certification guarantees the oil will maintain its good condition once it reaches store shelves.

We also use a range of options because we love to change things up and using a variety of oils keeps things fun. We enjoy the constant process of trying to find interesting oil, which inevitably brings the joy of meeting new producers, who become friends. And because olive oil is the product of agriculture and exhibits characteristics of its harvest year and terroir, the clock for seeking out new and exciting oil starts again every fall with each new harvest.

HOW TO BUY OLIVE OIL

In a perfect world, high quality extra-virgin olive oil would be affordable to all. But the reality is the best stuff costs money, often $50 a liter. This is inaccessible for daily use at home and would challenge a pizzeria's food costs. It's important to find oil that hits the freshness and flavor characteristics outlined below without breaking the bank.

With olive oil, freshness is paramount. Every production region has its own labeling requirements, but European olive oil may list the date of harvest. Get the freshest one you can find and afford. Also stick to oils that are made from olives from a single country (many Italian and Spanish companies, for example, bottle blended oils from three or four different countries, a sure sign they are commodity oils and those are never great). For domestic oil, there may not be a date of harvest listed on the label but there will be an expiration date. Use common sense to deduce which of the oils is most recently pressed by how far out the expiration date is. Ideally you want to use oil that is less than a year old. Old oil or oil that has been improperly stored in hot or sunny places becomes rancid. Unfortunately a lot of oil on the shelf, even that which has been recently pressed, is already rancid when you buy it, either due to poor production practices or storage issues, hence the need for taste testing to ensure quality.

If you get olive oil on your trip to Italy, use it up and don't save it for special occasions or it will go rancid. That said, I tend to not go out looking for Italian olive oil when I am shopping in America. There are plenty of expensive extra-virgin olive oils of super high quality, but the norm is unfortunately mediocre or low quality, the product of an industry rife with corruption and misleading labeling.

We prefer domestic oils from California. They are more affordable and, thanks to the wonderful technology they employ to harvest and process the fruit, the product can be extremely high quality. Plus, parts of California have unbelievable microclimates for olive cultivation, not unlike those of Italy or Spain. The mechanical methods that are used there to harvest olives keep the fruit healthy when harvested and the labor costs are very low, unlike in Italy, where most fruit is harvested by hand, which results in high labor costs, translating to higher costs for the consumer. Mechanical harvesting may also ensure the fruit reaches the press more quickly and efficiently than hand harvesting. Since fruit starts to degrade as soon as it's harvested, this time factor is critically important and reduces the likelihood the fruit will start fermenting before it is pressed, a phenomenon that leads to negative flavor attributes.

OLIVE OIL FLAVORS

My ideal olive oil has a perfect balance of fruitiness and bitterness with a gentle pungency and complex character. It should be free of defects such as flavors from fermentation, oxidation, and rancidity, and should have a pleasing texture and mouthfeel.

My ideal flavor profile might be very different than yours; I encourage you to explore the aromas and flavors in oil that appeal to you (as long as you're using quality extra-virgin olive oil void of defects; that's the only prerequisite).

I am a bit more forgiving with olive oil than tomato sauce due to its relatively minor role in pizza making. The most important things to avoid are oils with rancid or off flavors—and oils you don't like the taste of!

TASTING EXTRA-VIRGIN OLIVE OIL

At the restaurant, we approach olive oil tasting in a similar way to tomato sauce. We always judge it using the Olive Oil Evaluation Rubric (page 54) and keep track of our observations with detailed notes. Here's how we do it:

Step 1: Pour the olive oil into a glass bowl, ideally blue or black to mask the color. (This is a trick borrowed from professional tasters who don't want to be influenced by the oil's color because color is actually irrelevant to flavor.)

Step 2: Smell the olive oil by raising the bowl to your nose. Identify the aromas: Does it smell grassy, peppery, floral, herbal, fruity? If you can, name the aromas more specifically. Note if the oil smells off or rancid (like musty old fat, cardboard, or Play-Doh) or like alcohol. All of these negative attributes indicate flaws and will translate to negative flavors.

Step 3: Taste the olive oil. Roll the oil over your palate. Isolate its characteristics, positive and negative.

> **Negative flavor attributes:** Just as I do when I taste tomatoes, I look for negative flavor attributes first. Rancidity is the biggest issue that I encounter when tasting oils. So much oil on the market has the telltale signs of rancidity—the aromas mentioned above. Discard rancid oil. Note any "off" flavors or alcoholic notes caused by fruit that fermented before it made it to the press.

> **Positive flavor attributes:** This part is the most subjective. Although experts agree

that extra-virgin olive oil should taste like fresh olives with subtle grassy and fruity notes, personal preference for the range of flavors in the oil is up to you. My preference is for oils with notes like stone fruit and green apple. I look for complexity but I don't want anything that is too overpowering. I personally like nuanced and delicate oil. If your preference is for assertive flavors, go for it, especially if the pizza toppings can handle it.

Pungency: Peppery notes are good and indicate an oil is high quality and made from early harvest fruit. It gives a mild throat-burning sensation due to the natural presence of the phenolic compound and antioxidant oleocanthal.

Bitterness: There are two main sources of bitterness in oil and they are difficult to differentiate without practice. The positive source comes from oleuropein, a naturally occurring antioxidant in the fruit. Its presence is indicative of an early, healthy harvest. The other comes from rancidity and is disqualifying. If the bitterness is accompanied by rancid aromas, the source is rancidity. If the oil tastes clean and fresh in your mouth, the bitterness is from oleuropein.

Mouthfeel: Observe the texture of the oil on your lips and in your mouth. Obviously olive oil is oily but you don't want it to be overly greasy or leave an unpleasant fatty film behind. It should feel pure and clean with a dry finish.

CHEESE

Following tomatoes, cheese is the topping most closely associated with pizza. Most pizzerias use mozzarella in some form, but I love adding cheese of all sorts to my pies. I always consider first and foremost *when* to use it: before or after the bake. Get to know your melting cheeses and how they behave when heated on a pizza, and explore the world of fresh and delicate cheeses for adding afterward. In all cases, consider whether the cheese will add substantial fat or moisture to the pie (Parmigiano-Reggiano and Pecorino Romano, for example, do not), what flavors it brings to the mix, and how it will interact with other toppings.

FRESH MOZZARELLA

Mozzarella introduces flavor, moisture, and fat to your pizza. Pieces of raw mozzarella are distributed over the raw dough and toppings, which have their own moisture and fat content to consider. It's important to manage these factors individually and to take into consideration how they interact together, like in the case of acidic tomato sauce that mitigates the fattiness of the cheese. A very fatty mozzarella or one that is cut too small may melt too quickly and "break" (separate into an oily pool) on the pizza, while a very dry mozzarella may not properly melt, leaving lumps on the pie. Baking off a Test Pie (see page 171) is critical so you can make adjustments to the size and moisture of the cheese slice moving forward. The Mozzarella Evaluation Rubric (page 55) provides a framework for analyzing the cheese's characteristics.

Mozzarella is the most common topping cheese used in the recipes that follow, and on pizza in general. It is also one of the most temperamental toppings because it introduces a range of variables to your pizza like moisture, protein, and fat that affect its melting potential and the overall bake. One thing that I love about fresh mozzarella (called fior di latte in Italian and sometimes labeled as such in the U.S.) is that it changes from brand to brand and (for handmade cheese) from batch to batch. I don't mind a little inconsistency for artisanal products like this. Working with them just requires some trial and error when baking to make sure the cheese cut and temperature are right for that day's cheese.

How to Buy Mozzarella

Finding a high quality handmade mozzarella in your area may be one of the greatest sourcing challenges—and joys—you face. I have tasted hundreds of different mozzarellas over the years and the long journey has been frequently frustrating, as transport, freshness, and refrigeration can each have a negative impact on the flavor and texture of the mozzarella. The search for amazing fresh mozzarella can also be incredibly rewarding. Finding and tasting exceptional mozzarella can be transcendent. I speak from personal experience from when I discovered Jersey Girl Cheese in northern New Jersey, after inquiring about mozzarella cheese sources to the network of farmers and foragers I work with. If I hadn't been driven by a desire to find a handmade cheese made with milk from grass-fed cows, I never would have found their dreamy melter with ideal fat and moisture content—not to mention a connection and friendship with such a fantastic team.

Jersey Girl takes a very Italian artisanal approach to mozzarella making in which there are quite a few analogies to bread baking. They will be the first to tell you that there are two types of cow's milk mozzarella in the world: that which is eaten on its own drizzled with a bit of olive oil and that which can be torn or cut and melted on pizza.

The cheese made by artisan mozzarella makers is a different product altogether from the mass-produced low moisture brands (see page 34) sold in supermarkets. I don't typically use nationally available mozzarella brands except as a last resort because they are, by default, made in a factory, devoid of character, and intended to have a long shelf life—the antithesis of fresh mozzarella.

If you don't seek out or demand handmade fresh mozzarella in your community, it won't just magically appear. If you live in New Jersey or southern New York, you can purchase Jersey Girl mozzarella directly from their farm stand at Hillcrest Farm in Branchville, the shop in Rockaway, and farmers' markets in the area. Otherwise, I strongly suggest searching high and low for a source of fresh, handmade mozzarella near you. Speak to the cheese buyer in the deli department of your local supermarket and ask them if they can do better than the industrial brands. Create the demand.

Buffalo Mozzarella and Very High Moisture Mozzarella

Fresh buffalo mozzarella and very high moisture mozzarella made from cow's milk is best enjoyed raw. If you can get your hands on either, use them on the pizza after the bake, tearing pieces and distributing them evenly over the pie. This respects the integrity of the cheeses, which would otherwise be damaged by the oven's heat, and provides a pleasant temperature contrast between the hot pizza and room temperature cheese.

Most buffalo mozzarella in the United States is imported from Italy and no longer in its peak of freshness when it arrives. I haven't found a spectacular domestic source yet, so I don't use it on my pizzas.

How Artisanal Mozzarella Is Made

Jersey Girl and other artisanal mozzarella producers begin with fresh, raw, whole cow's milk, which they pasteurize and then combine with siero innesto, the bacteria-rich whey left over from the previous day's mozzarella making. This liquid is packed with a rich collection of bacteria; think of it as the starter culture in bread making. When the milk and bacteria-packed whey are combined and heated to about 100°F, the process activates protease enzymes similar to those activated when flour is mixed with water to make dough. The protease breaks down the milk's casein (a protein analogous to gluten in dough) the same way protease "cuts" gluten in pizza dough, influencing the extensibility and elasticity of the curds. The sliced proteins are now primed to bond with one another at a later step in the cheese making process when the cheese curds are kneaded—also

(Continued on page 34)

(Opposite and following) Scenes from making fresh mozzarella at Jersey Girl Cheese

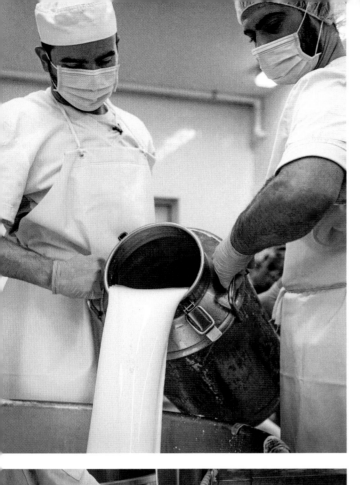

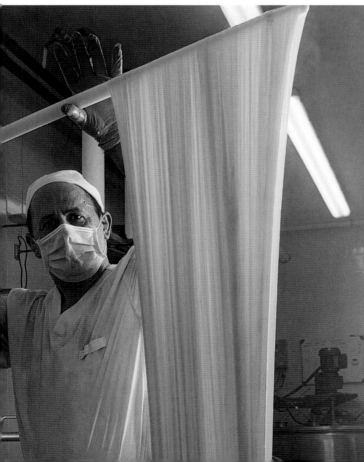
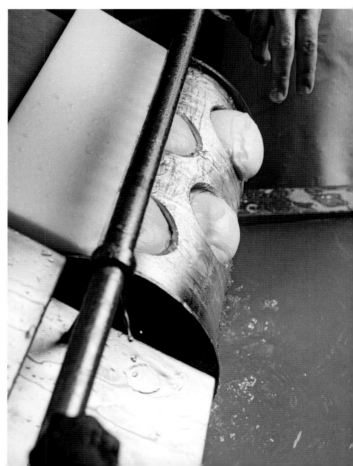

Low Moisture Mozzarella

Low moisture mozzarella is by far the most common mozzarella available in the U.S. It's sold in blocks called chubs, in hermetically sealed balls, and pre-shredded. Quality varies wildly and, although I don't use it on my pizzas, I am not opposed to using it if it's all you can find. Fresh mozzarella is always my first choice, but if you don't have access to it, low moisture mozzarella is a safe bet. Plus, growing up on the East Coast, I have a lot of nostalgia for it. It was used to top every favorite pizza of my youth.

Low moisture mozzarella is one of the great inventions of industrial food production. It transformed mozzarella, a fresh cheese with a short shelf life, into a shelf-stable product that can last for weeks or even months in the refrigerator. During the pulling process, most of the water is squeezed out of the cheese. The lack of moisture lends itself to a longer shelf life and the acidity level leads to a cheese structure that makes shredding, rather than tearing, the best choice for melting on a pizza. But this characteristic also leads it to melt more quickly, and ultimately "break" under prolonged heat exposure—that accounts for those greasy pools on New York slices.

Because it is always made in factories, low moisture mozzarella is subjected to plenty of analysis every step of the way so it is incredibly consistent from batch to batch. It's a reliable choice but not necessarily one that will give you the satisfaction of mastering the art of melting artisanal cheese. The ultra-pasteurization of the milk also robs the cheese of any real complexity, as the flavor compounds in the milk are destroyed in the process.

When judging low moisture mozzarella, don't apply the Mozzarella Evaluation Rubric. It will fail every time. But do keep in mind your slice size and breakage, only really able to be assessed after baking.

like gluten! Once the mixture cools, they add vegetable or animal rennet, a collection of enzymes that coagulates the milk proteins, separating the curds and whey. The curd-forming process takes about 3 hours (shorter in summer due to warmer temperatures, which accelerate the process, and longer in winter, when cooler temperatures slow it down).

Acidity is a major factor in the curds' readiness—and later it will influence the mozzarella's melting potential. Once the mixture reaches the target acidity range, the curds are ready to be cut and stretched. Some whey is drained, then the mixture is heated again with hot water and the curds are pulled into long ropes, elongating the proteins, then formed into a ball. This is the stage in which the casein proteins align to create their gluten-like network in the cheese.

The key during this step as it relates to the pizza making process is to stay within the target acidity and temperature range and not lose too much moisture and fat as the curds are pulled and squeezed. All have to be in perfect balance so the finished cheese melts properly. A fatty mozzarella melts better without breaking or burning in the oven than one with a lower fat content. To guarantee the mozzarella will not be too moist and leave a milky puddle behind as it melts later, just the right moisture is squeezed out before it is formed into balls. This is regulated by the touch of the cheesemaker. The final product feels moist and springy.

We receive regular deliveries from Jersey Girl and, although their product is fairly consistent, we always run a Test Pie with the mozzarella, baking off a pie with cheese from that day's delivery before service, to see how it melts. Even tiny variations in moisture and fat content will impact the outcome from day to day—more flowy one day, more resistant to melting the next. Even the very same ball of cheese, if cut in two and used on two different days, will behave differently each day, because fresh cheese is still living in a way and changing moment to moment.

TASTING FRESH MOZZARELLA

Before you begin discerning the proper size for tearing and cutting mozzarella for melting on a pizza, you have to find a quality product. If you cannot find a great handmade mozzarella, use store-bought. Regardless of your source, be sure to assess the cheese's characteristics using the Mozzarella Evaluation Rubric (page 55). Judgment criteria include color, flavor, texture, mouthfeel, heat tolerance, and flow/melt.

Color: Slice the ball of mozzarella in half and examine the color of the cheese's skin and interior. My ideal mozzarella comes from grass-fed cows and has a yellowish or off-white color. Some color variation is fine: the color of the cow's milk depends on what they eat; milk from grass-fed cows, for example, produces milk (and therefore cheese) with a yellow tint.

Texture: Examine the cross-section and observe the interior of the cheese and how compact, dry, or juicy it is. The texture, both to the touch as well as in your mouth, should be soft, creamy, and luxurious and it should spring back when poked. Note if the texture is more compact or drier in the center of the slice versus the edges. If it's dry, you may need to soak the cheese in a bit of milk or cream to reconstitute it before using to compensate for the lack of moisture, a trick I learned from J. Kenji López-Alt. Simply tear or cut the mozzarella into 1-inch pieces, then soak for 20 minutes and drain before using.

Flavor: The mozzarella should have a distinct milk flavor. It should taste buttery, rich, and very slightly acidic. A cheese made from grazing cows will have complex flavors like grass and hay with bold lactic notes. Taste for salt. The cheese should taste slightly briny.

Mouthfeel: Taste the raw cheese and assess the moisture and fat content and how it feels in your mouth. When your teeth bite through it, does the moisture fill your cheeks? Does it resist your teeth as you bite into it? If so, how much? Is it grainy? Does it feel dry? A cheese that excretes a lot of liquid may be too wet for pizza making (though if you set it aside for a day or two out of its brine it will become drier and perhaps

Controlling Cheese Flow

Some cheeses are very efficient melters. To control the flow, alternate dollops of cheese and dollops of sauce over the surface of the dough. The cheese being in direct contact with the dough (as opposed to riding on top of the tomato) will offer some resistance to the flow, slowing it down.

Cutting Cheese

When you make your first pizza, only tear and cut as much cheese as you need for that one pie. Distribute the 1-inch pieces over the dough and bake. Observe how the cheese melts, flows, and tolerates heat, then customize the size of the cheese slice for future pies accordingly. If the cheese melts too quickly and breaks, cut and tear the cheese into larger than 1¼- to 1½-inch pieces. If the cheese doesn't melt well, use ¾-inch pieces.

more adapted to melting on a pizza without leaving excess liquid behind). A very juicy cheese, if used in the quantity listed in the recipes that follow, might be too wet, so bake a Test Pie with it and if it leaves a puddle on the pizza, bake the next pie with 5 grams less.

Heat tolerance: Proteins in the cheese are the "glue" that holds it together. When they are heated, they break down and the cheese melts. If the cheese is subjected to high temperatures over a prolonged period it may "break," or separate into an oily puddle before the pizza has finished baking. Bake time and temperature will determine how the cheese melts, and once it is melted, if it cooks too long, whether it breaks. A cheese is properly melted when it oozes but doesn't separate. The best way to remedy breaking is to tear or cut the cheese into larger pieces, which melt more slowly so they have more time in the heat of the oven to get those desirable little brown spots of caramelization without separating.

Mozzarella has a life cycle of sorts, and its proteins and moisture content—and therefore its ability to flow—change over time. It melts differently the day it is "born" versus a day or two later. All three stages are workable, you just have to know how to make adjustments. Fresher mozzarella tends to flow more freely so you can use less of it than day-old cheese to achieve similar results. On the other hand, a day-old mozzarella may need to be soaked in warm milk or cream to bring it to an ideal moisture level for melting on a pizza.

Fresh cheese

Day-old cheese

Flow/melt: Alternatively, increase the moisture and fat content of the cheese by soaking it in warm milk or cream. The size of the cheese and its quality massively impact cheese flow and how long cheese can stay in the oven. When I'm making pizza at home, whether it's in a low temperature oven where the pizza is going to be in the oven for 6 or 7 minutes or in a wood fired oven, which only takes a few minutes, my goal is the same: for the cheese to flow onto the pizza and in/on the sauce but not leave liquid pools in its wake. I always start with 1-inch torn or cut pieces, bake a pie, then judge which adjustments are needed based on how the cheese melts. Ideally I want some rosy color where the melted cheese and tomato sauce meet. When the pizza comes out of the oven, I look for maximum flow.

OTHER MELTING CHEESES

Like mozzarella, other melting cheeses introduce flavor, moisture, and fat to your pizza. Apply the mozzarella tasting criteria to any cheeses you want to put on a pizza as long as they are good melters. Avoid cheeses that don't melt, like goat cheese, but don't rule out putting them on after the bake. Choose a cheese you like, slice to a size that matches up with your oven temperature (start at 1 inch and work up or down in size according to how it melts on top of your Test Pie, and whether it breaks). Don't be afraid to blend two cheeses together, half mozzarella, half scamorza, for example. And don't feel confined to the world of Italian or domestic cheeses. Raclette, Gruyère, and Emmental are all great melters!

Fontina

Fontina is a wonderful washed rind cheese from the Italian Alpine region of Valle d'Aosta. It's soft when raw, and flowy when melted, conjuring thoughts of northern Italian fonduta. It adds a decadent richness to the Bosco (page 213), but I could see it on the Bianca (page 208) as well. Alternatively, omit the scamorza from the Funghi (page 182) and add fontina. The cheese works well on white pies.

Fontina production is governed by strict rules that limit its zone of production, so it's one of the imported ingredients in the book that you won't be able to source locally unless you live in Italy. If you'd prefer a domestic cheese, try Cherry Grove Farm's Buttercup Brie, triple cream cow's milk cheese, or any soft and funky washed rind cheese.

Scamorza

Scamorza belongs to the mozzarella universe of Italian cheese styles. It is typically made from cow's milk and the curd is stretched and formed into balls like mozzarella, but the cheese is aged for at least two weeks, which impacts its texture, rendering it compact and springy. The texture is medium-dry, similar to that of low moisture mozzarella, and it melts best when shredded. It pairs well with mozzarella and appears alongside it on the Corn (page 181) and Funghi (page 182) pizzas.

OTHER CHEESES AND DAIRY

This category encompasses a wide range of dairy toppings, from silky ricotta to savory aged Parmigiano-Reggiano. Some go on before the bake so they melt and mingle with the other toppings, others after, acting as a sort of seasoning to the cooked toppings. Regardless of whether the ingredient goes on before or after the bake, always taste it in its raw form and determine how best to utilize it without losing its prime characteristics. Assess its richness, seasoning, and texture before determining how to pair it, what size to slice or dollop it, and whether it should be cooked or raw.

Burrata

Burrata's name is a bit misleading; its root is *burro* ("butter" in Italian) but it's really the cousin of mozzarella. It is made by heating and stretching curds, forming them into a parcel, then stuffing said parcel with cream and shredded curds. The flavor should be milky, sweetly lactic, and fresh. Due to the fact that a lot of burrata sold in the U.S. is imported from Italy, it's not fresh when it hits your table, so it has developed overly acidic flavors. If your burrata is tangy or sour, it's already way past its prime.

A good, fresh burrata has a thin "shell" that is easy to chew through, tender yet with a slightly springy structure, much like a stellar mozzarella you would find in Italy. There's a lot more richness and moisture to burrata than to mozzarella, however. When you break a parcel of burrata open it should be creamy and moist but not super liquidy. If it is very loose and watery, I won't use it on a pizza to avoid making the crust super soggy. It's best for pizza when it's on the firmer side and not as flowy.

I never put burrata on a pizza before the bake for two reasons. The first is crucial to preserving the integrity of the flavor and structure: Heating burrata mellows the flavor and melts the curds, depriving them of their unique "burrata-ness." Second, I love the contrast of a hot pizza with a cool, creamy cheese.

Burrata pairs extraordinarily well with tomatoes, which bring their own sweetness, plus the tomatoes provide an acidic contrast that cuts through the fat. Burrata adds richness to anything you put it on, so any burrata pizza you freestyle should take that into account. When approaching the complementary toppings, I avoid adding those with too much fat. Anchovies, prosciutto, and Brussels sprouts work great. Due to its high fat content, pepperoni won't be a home run unless you're really capable of digesting that much heaviness.

Ricotta

Ricotta isn't technically cheese. It's made by heating inoculated whey after cheese making, then collecting the resulting fine curd. In Italy, ricotta's ancestral home, it is often served on its own, drizzled with olive oil with a side of toasted bread. I like this approach and when I use ricotta, I typically leave it raw and allow its delicate flavors to shine through by avoiding overpowering toppings.

Every supermarket dairy aisle stocks plastic containers of ricotta, often sporting a shelf life of several months due to added preservatives. The consistency can be watery or granular and the flavor quite bland. Your best bet for getting excellent ricotta is to purchase it from a small local dairy farm if you're lucky enough to know one. That's where you're most likely to find ricotta as it should be: tender, light, airy, with a super delicate essence of milk.

Ricotta Salata

Ricotta salata is fresh ricotta that has been dried, then salted and aged, to preserve it. The addition of salt draws out the moisture and changes the structure of the ricotta, making it more compact and grate-able. Depending on the producer, it can be on the assertive side in terms of tanginess and may have a saltier exterior than interior. Be sure to taste it in wedges, which will give the full spectrum of saltiness, from the rind to the heart, before using.

Parmigiano-Reggiano

Parmigiano-Reggiano is an Italian cow's milk cheese and should not be confused with Parmesan, a grating cheese that can be made just about anywhere. The former is made in a strictly defined and limited zone around Parma, Italy, according to historic practices. Parmigiano-Reggiano is delightfully granular, savory, and rich. It is a terrific grating cheese and, unless a pizza has a lot of liquid on it for the cheese to "melt" into like the Pork Pie (page 224), I don't add it before the bake. Instead, I rely on its savory notes to season a pizza after the bake.

There is a spectrum of quality grades to Parmigiano-Reggiano and relative quality is reflected in the price. I recommend finding an accessible Parmigiano-Reggiano. Don't go crazy and use 36-month aged cheese made from the milk of heritage Vacche Rosse ("red cows"). Look for an 18-month standard Parm and save anything more precious for eating on its own to savor its complexity. Though it's not as prestigious as Parmigiano-Reggiano, Grana Padano makes a fine substitute and has some of the same nutty and savory notes.

The ideal fineness for grated cheese varies, depending on the timing and your intention. When I put it on before cooking like on the Pork Pie (page 224) or the Meatball (page 229), I want a super-fine grate like the one you get from the punched holes

of a box grater. If the cheese goes on after cooking, I like to use a Microplane with pretty wide holes so you get a fine flake. One's a dusting and the other is a flurry. We want the fine grate to melt into any moisture on the pizza since Parmigiano-Reggiano doesn't melt on its own. The flurry after the bake settles into crevices and seasons the toppings. It's wonderful to shave curls over the arugula on the Montagna (page 207) as the size and shape of the curls match the other raw topping, arugula leaves. A finely grated cheese would get lost in the pile of greens.

Pecorino Romano

Pecorino Romano is a salted sheep's milk cheese named for the Italian capital but produced in a vast area that encompasses the entire region of Lazio, the island of Sardinia, and the southernmost province of Tuscany. In Rome, local production tends to be very heavily salted, while exported Pecorino Romano seems bland in comparison. I like to use it as a finely grated flurry to finish a pizza and I always taste it in advance to gauge the saltiness before further

seasoning the pie. Pecorino is available everywhere. Buy the best you can afford.

Vegan Alternatives

I don't have deep experience baking with vegan cheese alternatives, but if that's your jam, go for it! Just keep the lessons imparted in this chapter in mind. Another option is to omit the cheese in dairy-based recipes to make them vegan.

Crispy Cheese Crust

Try grating Parmigiano-Reggiano or Pecorino Romano over the raised border of the raw dough to create a textural component to the crust. As it bakes, the cheese will break and make the crust a little bit crispy.

CURED MEATS

Pepperoni, prosciutto, guanciale, speck, and any other cured meat you wish to add are going to bring a level of savoriness and seasoning to your pizza. They may also deliver a healthy dose of fat. Keep these factors in mind when selecting your cured meat of choice.

It's not hard to find pepperoni sticks; it is a greater challenge to track down natural pepperoni. This is where reading the label is essential. If you can, purchase pepperoni made only with pork, salt, and natural seasonings. Otherwise, get pepperoni with as few additives as possible and always with a natural casing. We prefer stick pepperoni so we can control the thickness. Using a deli slicer and

caliper, we tried ten different thicknesses and determined that pepperoni sliced to a thickness of 1.75 to 2 millimeters provided the textural component of caramelization around the edges so it curls and cups nicely, provides the proper mouthfeel (maintaining integrity but easy to chew through), and is fully cooked in the time we bake a pie. Dialing in the thickness of pepperoni and other cured meats with a caliper ensures they cook predictably every time, but we don't want them so thin that they melt onto the pizza and get lost. Any cured meat is ripe for pizza topping as long as the slice is right. Assess whether to put it on before or after cooking, and then contrast its fattiness with the acidic components of the pizza, such as tomato sauce.

In Praise of the Caliper

I used to think that using a caliper to measure the thickness of slices of guanciale or garlic was a geeky move. But the more I developed my vision for the ideal pizza, the more I realized it is actually an essential tool for nailing the perfect thickness of something that needs to melt onto or cook through on a pizza at

a specific temperature for a given period of time. Even changing an ingredient's thickness by 0.5 millimeter can make it more pleasant (or more difficult!) to eat. At just $10, a caliper is an affordable instrument for managing your toppings and ensuring consistency from one bake to the next.

ONIONS
1-2 mm

FENNEL
1-1.5 mm

PEPPERONI
1.75-2 mm

GUANCIALE
0.8 mm

PRODUCE

I use produce as fresh raw toppings or deeply flavored roasted toppings, depending on which approach accentuates the wonderful flavors and textures of nature.

Agriculture is all around us. Whether I am at home in view of a cornfield or in Jersey City, where rooftop urban gardens offer views of the New York skyline, I see the undeniable evidence that food can grow anywhere. While the vast amount of agriculture in the U.S. is done on an industrial scale—a byproduct of many forces—there are small farms on every corner of the map. To find one near you, visit a farmers' market and talk to the vendors about their produce. Ask your friends, neighbors, teachers, and librarians where they get their fruits and vegetables. I have found that some of the most talented farmers get the word out through word of mouth so a Google search might not turn up a very cool place near you.

If you have a public park nearby or a yard at your home, there are many wild things out there for the taking. Some of the items that grow in my backyard like dandelion greens, garlic mustard, and pea tendrils influence my pizza toppings. I can walk through a park by my house and find Japanese knotweed and black walnuts (still haven't put those on a pizza yet, but I'm not ruling anything out!). The moral of the story is agriculture is everywhere and anywhere. Your location and climate determine what you have access to locally, which is why I let nature decide my toppings—and cooking in general. I may go to a farmers' market or to a farm directly to see what's out there. I trade pizza for produce from my neighbor's backyard; I highly recommend this as a method of commerce. I even try to grow some of my own fruits and vegetables. In all cases, I use what is the freshest and tastes the most delicious at the moment and consider how it might pair best alongside other toppings.

I could write a whole book just about how my approach to a single type of produce changes throughout its season. But I think it is more useful to provide thoughtful notes and guidelines on how we use toppings after assessing their texture and flavor, how an item's moment in the season might affect its character on a pizza, and how its size should be managed so it eats nicely.

In other words, we avoid basing our pizza toppings on our whims—sure, we'd love a roasted corn pizza in the dead of winter, but the tasteless, out-of-season corn won't bring us the same joy as the flavors of an in-season winter squash pie.

The book's last section features toppings that highlight seasonal produce. Because Razza is in New Jersey, the toppings in the recipes in Part 4 very much reflect the availability of produce in the Northeast. But even more important than having a recipe blueprint for how to prepare toppings, we think it's critical to understand why a certain topping is fitting, how it should be prepared (cooked, sliced) before being put on the pizza, its proportional relationship to the other ingredients, and why you are using it at any moment in its season. You can extrapolate from the lessons in the pages that follow and apply them when modifying your own pizza toppings or just shopping and cooking produce for other dishes.

ASSESSING PRODUCE

There are four factors that determine how we use produce on our pizzas: texture, flavor, size, and season.

Texture: This category encompasses a wide range of possibilities, including moisture content, density, and the physical makeup of an ingredient.

Flavor: Consider an ingredient's flavor profile, its acidity (or lack thereof), whether it tastes better raw or cooked, and how it might complement or clash with another topping, then prepare it accordingly.

Size: Ask yourself how the dimensions of an ingredient can positively or negatively impact its use. Slice some toppings so they are thin enough to cook on the pizza but not so thin that they get lost (a caliper comes in handy for dialing this in, see page 40). Cut other toppings into pieces that are easy to navigate in one bite.

Season: Learn how produce behaves at every point in its season and determine how best to harness its potential. Taste everything.

The first step is to taste an ingredient and assess its texture: Is the chicory stalk tough, are the peas or corn starchy, is the basil limp? In the case of chicory, blanching for a short time in boiling water softens the stalk and makes it easier to bite through when it's time to take a bite of your pizza. For corn, blanching the kernels hydrates the starch and keeps the pellicle (outer sheath) super thin, making the cooked product more pleasant to eat. If basil is limp or becoming black around the edges, it may no longer be suitable for use.

Next, we assess the flavor profile: Is the chicory pleasantly bitter, are the peas or corn very sweet, is the basil herbaceous? Seasonings like salt, chili, and oil must be customized in both quantity and flavor profile to best balance or complement the other toppings.

Size is another important factor. A pea is already in its ready-to-eat form, but a squash must be diced to make each piece bite sized. Consider the best way to preserve or change an ingredient size to make it easier to eat without compromising its integrity.

Finally, the point in the season may affect the flavor, texture, and size of the produce. Young peas are a perfect topping, but once they show signs of starchiness, we no longer use them, as their tender texture has passed. We love using produce in season, while acknowledging that not every point in a plant's life cycle offers the characteristics we look for in its use.

CORN

Corn may seem like an unlikely pizza topping, but when treated thoughtfully it can make a delicious protagonist on a pie. Arriving at the Razza Corn Pie (page 181) was a process. We ran trials with roasted corn, contrasting kernels roasted on and off the cob. We tried boiling, sautéing, and putting kernels on the pizza raw. After eight summers of experimentation, we determined that boiling corn cobs maintains the kernels' shape, while rendering their pellicle tender and helping them reach peak plumpness. When you slice boiled kernels off the cob and put them on a pizza before the bake, the result is a really succulent final product with all the sweetness and plumpness of summer corn on the cob.

FENNEL

Fennel is surprisingly versatile with a very long life cycle. You can start by using its microgreens (the first sprouts of fennel) like an herb, exploiting the anise flavor to accent squash or mushroom pies. The first small bulbs are tender and sweet, while later in the season they grow fibrous. Shave young fennel thin enough to cook through when distributed raw over a pizza. Dice and roast more mature bulbs to soften their texture and tease out pleasing caramelized flavors. Sprinkle the mature fronds onto a cooked pie, or blend them into pesto. When the fennel flowers, harvest the flowers and pollen and employ after the bake for a pop of fennel flavor. You can even harvest the fennel seeds and use them in the sausage for the Santo (page 211)— or plant in your garden.

ZUCCHINI

Zucchini, and squash in general, are among the most abundant summer fruits in New Jersey. We can get them from late spring to early fall and the size and texture transform dramatically through the seasons. It's very exciting to get the first squashes after a long winter, but by the end of summer, we're pretty much over it. And that's fine, because what we are really looking for in zucchini is the tenderness and tiny seeds of a young fruit. By mid to late season, zucchini start to develop watery seed pockets with an unpleasant texture, and removing them is an added step that doesn't really work for a restaurant with a small prep space. For a home cook, it just generates waste and you end up paying for the inner part of the zucchini, which is discarded. Plus, if you remove the seeds, you lose the beautiful coin-like circular slice.

When choosing zucchini, look for fruit that is 6 to 8 inches long and an inch or so in diameter so the slices are a consistent size. Due to its high water content and relatively subtle flavor, zucchini should be salted in advance. The salt causes the zucchini to release some of their liquid, while also seasoning them. This process eliminates moisture, which would otherwise dampen the pie. It also concentrates the flavor of the zucchini and tenderizes the flesh so they cook properly during the bake. Cut the zucchini, weigh them,

and immediately salt them with 0.75 percent salt by weight. Then let sit overnight and drain and squeeze off any excess water. Using the Cook's Percentages approach (see page 185) offers a reliable way to accurately season slices every time.

FRESH TOMATOES

Tomato sauce made with whole canned peeled tomatoes (see page 243) is a year-round ingredient and we only really use fresh tomatoes for sauce when they are in peak season, from July through September. Avoid out-of-season tomatoes or any fruit that is grainy, under-ripe, or mealy.

Always use tomatoes with the ideal moisture content or you will end up with a damp pizza. Sauce made from heirloom tomatoes tends to contain far too much moisture without additional straining. Let such sauce sit in a fine mesh strainer for a couple of hours so you don't end up with a watery pizza. Use the fresh sauce to replace sauce from canned tomatoes for pies like the Rossa (page 173) and Burrata (page 178). Bake the sauce onto a Test Pie (page 171) and make any adjustments to its consistency with the next pizza. Like sauce made from whole canned peeled tomatoes, you will only know if fresh tomato sauce is the right consistency after baking it.

Another option is to put fresh chopped tomatoes on a white pizza (one without tomato sauce). In this case, the tomato acts as a topping instead of a sauce. We don't mind the texture of thin tomato skins, so we don't bother blanching and peeling, just slice the tomatoes straight away. I avoid any varieties that have a very thick skin like plum or San Marzano (though they work well for Fresh Tomato Sauce, page 244).

To determine the size, we let the tomato do the dictating. Something really small like a Sungold or Super Sweet 100 can go on the pizza whole. For large varieties like Brandywine, we cut out any spots that are green, brown, or hard. That variety has a lot of inedible parts so we just focus on using the most tender bits on the pie. If we have Green Zebra or Garden Peach heirloom varieties, they look beautiful sliced crosswise into rounds and distributed like pepperoni.

ARUGULA

The flavor of arugula is hugely variable, depending on the season, the species, and the method of cultivation. It ranges from the super delicate winter arugula grown on hydroponic farms to the intensely peppery wild summer varieties. To maintain its herbaceous vegetal flavors, we put it on raw after the bake but only if the leaves and stalks are tender. Once they turn fibrous, we blend them into Spring Pesto (page 251) for a peppery bite.

MUSHROOMS

Mushrooms are available year-round, but in the height of summer we take a step back because there is so much else coming out of the ground. The rest of the year, we collaborate with a local forager, Dan Lipow, who we trust to supply the goods for our seasonal mushroom pizza. The varieties change regularly; two weeks a year we have morels, then chanterelles and maitakes. Having a mushroom forager sounds like an elite luxury, but I would wager that there's at least one person in your area who fills this role for local markets and restaurants—or does it just out of passion. Check with your local farmers' market vendors, farm to table chef, or Asian produce market to access the rotating variety of mushrooms available near you.

Mushrooms have a very high water content, which is a major factor to contend with. If you use them raw on your pizza, they will likely leave a puddle on the pie. The amount of moisture is influenced by the type of mushroom, how it's cultivated, and the point in its life cycle. We don't typically use raw mushrooms on a pizza. We roast them beforehand to let the mushrooms release their liquid (save those juices for a soup!) and to bring out really nice caramelized flavors. The key is to tear or cut them into bite sized pieces before roasting so they are easy to navigate with each bite.

PEAS

There are some peas that are so good, you shouldn't even bother heating them on a pizza. Eat them raw straight out of the pod and find another topping. I'm mostly kidding, but when I get a really stellar harvest, all I want to do is press pause on my day and eat peas right from the shell.

Peas, like most produce, develop throughout their season. They are sweet and tender at the beginning of spring and as the season progresses they become starchy and less sweet. As soon as they lose their initial sweetness and tender texture, we don't use them any longer. If you grow your own, garnish your pizza with tender pea tendrils.

HAZELNUTS

Hazelnuts are an unusual pizza topping but an exciting one, offering a New Jersey connection alongside amazing flavor and a nice textural surprise. We soak them to prevent burning, then distribute over the pizza with ricotta and honey (page 196), which plays on the nuts' natural sweetness.

You can technically use hazelnuts all year—packaged varieties are always on store shelves—but due to their high fat content they start to degrade and go rancid (just like olive oil) as they age, so we use them just after they are harvested in the fall. The particular hazelnut we use is a blight-resistant variety developed by Rutgers (see Project Hazelnut box, opposite), which has a very high fat content and a full, rich flavor. You can take the same approach with any nut or seed that inspires you. If you have black walnuts in your backyard like I do, figure out how to get them out of the shell and use them.

PUMPKIN AND WINTER SQUASH

You can use any edible pumpkin or winter squash (avoid ornamental gourds and spaghetti squash, though). Just as with meatier mushroom varieties, I like the texture and caramelized flavor of roasted squash on my pizza. Cooking in advance is essential, as squash won't cook through in the short time the pizza is in the oven. Winter squash have so much sugar and the best way to really bring out all that sweetness and nice flavor is to roast them.

Roasty flavors and caramelization are also very adapted to a winter palate.

We peel the squash, cut it into the desired size (usually ½-inch dice), then drizzle with olive oil, season with salt, and roast at 425°F until it is cooked through and 90 percent caramelized, about 40 minutes. It will cook the rest of the way on the pizza. You can also use whole roasted squash leftovers.

BRUSSELS SPROUTS

Brussels sprouts had a moment some years back. After dwelling in a realm of boiled vegetables and childhood nightmares, home cooks discovered how to prepare them in a way that accentuated their flavors—roasting to the point of deep caramelization. We love when we start getting Brussels delivered, Ping-Pong -ball-sized green globes clinging to long stalks, one of the most endearingly bizarre-looking plants out there.

Ours come straight from the farm, picked and delivered fresh. When you're looking for your own, you'll likely encounter them separated from their stalks and packaged. The key is to buy fresh sprouts, with better flavor and complexity than old ones, which get black and brown spots, yellowed leaves, and a shriveled look. They store well, so you can get them deep into the winter, but they won't be as fresh as the fall ones. A fresh one almost squeaks when you squeeze it and its leaves are tightly wrapped. Once the leaves start to come loose, the sprout is past its prime.

Peel off the outer layers and set aside, then once you have revealed the heart, where the leaves are too tight to peel off, shave them on a mandoline. The two contrasting textures of the whole outer leaves and sliced inner heart make a wonderful pizza topping that works well with Melted Anchovies (page 221) and Garlic Confit (page 249) or with cured pork like guanciale or pancetta.

Project Hazelnut

There's a worldwide hazelnut shortage thanks to the meteoric success of hazelnut products like Nutella. In fact Ferrero, the Italy-based company that produces Nutella and Ferrero Rocher has contributed in no small way to depleting the world's hazelnut stock, as well as investing in monoculture—the cultivation of a single variety—with large scale plantation projects in Turkey and Italy.

Hazelnuts in modern commercial times have become synonymous with Italian products, but not long ago, hazelnut trees bearing heirloom varieties thrived across the globe, including in New Jersey. A project at Rutgers, the state university of New Jersey, has been dedicated to reviving and improving upon these forgotten trees for the past twenty-five years. Dr. Tom Molnar, a friend of mine from Cook College, Rutgers's agriculture school, is the head breeder running the project.

The aim of the project is to breed a nut that is resistant to Eastern Filbert Blight, a fungal disease that affects hazelnut trees and once wiped out the East Coast population, as well as to develop new agricultural opportunities and markets for local farmers. The process is a slow and methodical one in which farmers take the best nuts, study them, then replant them. It takes about five years for a crop to begin fruiting. Now there are 10,000 trees statewide and we commit to buying fruit from them each year. It's a fun and rewarding collaboration that we look forward to every fall.

Combining Ingredients

We typically approach the combination of toppings by selecting one seasonal produce star and two supporting cast members. We taste the toppings raw and try

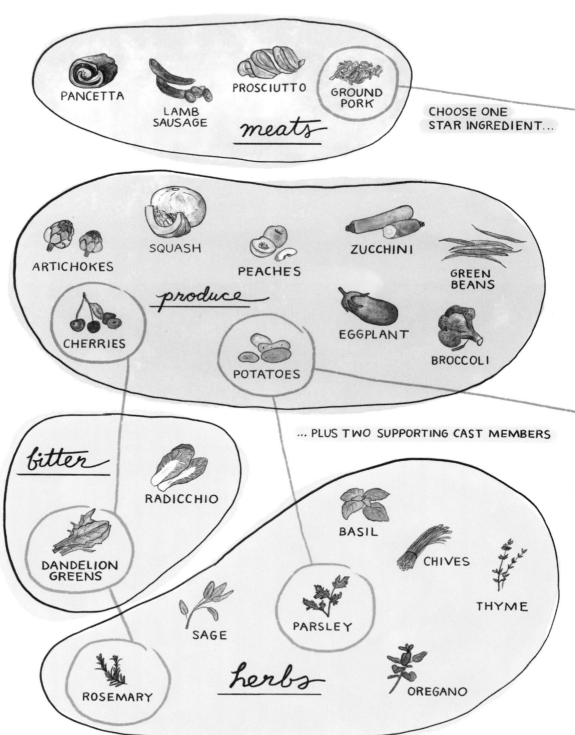

PANCETTA

LAMB SAUSAGE

PROSCIUTTO

GROUND PORK

meats

CHOOSE ONE STAR INGREDIENT...

ARTICHOKES

SQUASH

produce

PEACHES

ZUCCHINI

GREEN BEANS

CHERRIES

EGGPLANT

POTATOES

BROCCOLI

... PLUS TWO SUPPORTING CAST MEMBERS

bitter

RADICCHIO

DANDELION GREENS

BASIL

CHIVES

THYME

SAGE

PARSLEY

herbs

ROSEMARY

OREGANO

to envision how they will interact with one another, considering the need for some sort of acidic component.

heat
FRESNO
HABANERO
BLACK PEPPER
CRUSHED RED PEPPER

savory! umami
BONITO FLAKES
ANCHOVIES
BOTTARGA

crispy
ALMONDS
PINE NUTS
BREADCRUMBS
FRIED ONIONS
HAZELNUTS

sweet
RAISINS
GARLIC CONFIT
MAPLE SYRUP
HONEY

acid
LEMON
OTHER CITRUS
VINEGAR

creamy/rich
BRIE
HEAVY CREAM
MASCARPONE
RACLETTE

RUBRICS

Use the rubrics alongside the tasting instructions for whole canned tomatoes, extra-virgin olive oil, and fresh mozzarella in the preceding pages to determine which brand of each has the best possible flavors and characteristics for you to use on your pizzas. Evaluate multiple brands in a blind tasting: Label each sample with a number and use each chart to record your observations based on the numbered statements. The sample with the highest score is the one that you should use on your pizzas. Scan the QR codes beside each rubric to download and print additional rubrics.

TOMATO EVALUATION RUBRIC

SCAN FOR RUBRIC

As discussed in the Tasting Tomatoes section in the preceding pages (see page 20), our ideal tomato is bright red in color with a perfect balance of sweetness and acidity with the original and pure tomato flavor intact.

1 = Statement is not true at all
2 = Statement is barely true but mostly wrong
3 = Statement is somewhat true but neutral
4 = Statement is mostly true but not perfect
5 = Statement is completely true and accurate

A. Color
1. Has a bright, vibrant, and ripe red color
2. Is not dull and rusty or white/green/yellow

B. Viscosity
1. Includes actual tomato flesh
2. Is not watery
3. Is not overly concentrated or paste-like

C. Texture and mouthfeel
1. Is close to biting into a ripe, raw tomato
2. Is velvety and luscious
3. Is not watery
4. Is not hard or firm

D. Seeds and skins
1. Has the least amount of seeds
2. Has the least amount of skin

E. Positive flavor attributes (not sweetness or acidity)
1. Has ripe tomato flavor
2. Flavor is close to an actual fresh tomato
3. Could eat these tomatoes right out of the can
4. There are no off flavors
5. Flavor is clean and pure
6. Has no flavors of fermentation

F. Acidity
1. Is a bright and lively tomato
2. Will not produce heartburn after eating (excess acidity)
3. The acidity is evident but balanced
4. Does not have vinegar notes

G. Sweetness
1. There is a balanced sweetness
2. Does not taste like sugar
3. Has inherent natural sweetness like ripe fruit

	SAMPLE 1	SAMPLE 2	SAMPLE 3	SAMPLE 4	SAMPLE 5	SAMPLE 6	SAMPLE 7
A. Color							
B. Viscosity							
C. Texture							
D. Seeds/skins							
E. Flavor							
F. Acidity							
G. Sweetness							
Total							
Average							

Add up the numbers in each column and divide by 7. The sample with the highest number is the one you should use.

Notes: _____ _____ _____

_____ _____ _____

_____ _____ _____

OLIVE OIL EVALUATION RUBRIC

SCAN FOR RUBRIC

Blind-taste oil according to the Tasting Extra-Virgin Olive Oil section (see page 26) in the preceding pages. Our ideal olive oil has a perfect balance of fruitiness and bitterness with a gentle pungency and full character. It should be free of defects such as flavors from fermentation and oxidation. Color and viscosity should not be major factors in tasting.

1=Statement is not true at all
2=Statement is barely true but mostly wrong
3=Statement is somewhat true but neutral
4=Statement is mostly true but not perfect
5=Statement is completely true and accurate

A. Pungency

1. Has a peppery, throat-burning sensation due to the oleocanthal (indicative of early harvest oils)

B. Positive flavor attributes (character)

1. It has a fruity taste
   a. Taste is reminiscent of stone fruit such as peaches
   b. Taste is reminiscent of green apple
2. It has grassy notes
3. It has herbaceous notes
4. Smells and tastes like fresh fruit growing on a tree

C. Texture and mouthfeel

1. Has a dry and clean finish
2. Does not leave your mouth feeling greasy
3. Is clean and pure

D. Bitterness

1. Has a slight bitterness from the oleuropein (indicative of early harvest oils)

E. Negative flavor attributes (defects)

1. Does not have off flavors due to fermentation (late harvest/old olives)
2. Does not smell or taste like alcohol
3. Does not smell or taste oxidized or rancid

	SAMPLE 1	SAMPLE 2	SAMPLE 3	SAMPLE 4	SAMPLE 5	SAMPLE 6	SAMPLE 7
A. Pungency							
B. Character							
C. Texture							
D. Bitterness							
E. Defects							
Total							
Average							

Add up the numbers in each column and divide by 5. The sample with the highest number is the one you should use.

Notes: _____   _____   _____
_____   _____   _____
_____   _____   _____

MOZZARELLA
EVALUATION RUBRIC

SCAN FOR RUBRIC

Blind-taste cheese brands according to the Tasting Fresh Mozzarella section (see page 34) in the preceding pages. Our ideal cheese is off-white in color with a perfect balance of richness and milk flavor and a soft, creamy, luxurious texture.

1=Statement is not true at all
2=Statement is barely true but mostly wrong
3=Statement is somewhat true but neutral
4=Statement is mostly true but not perfect
5=Statement is completely true and accurate

A. Color
1. Is yellowish, off-white
2. Is not bright white or bleached-looking

B. Heat tolerance
1. Has a long window of heat exposure without breaking

C. Texture and mouthfeel
1. Offers minimal resistance, is soft and luxurious
2. Is not rubbery, mealy, or dry
3. Is easy and pleasurable to chew through

D. Positive flavor attributes (character)
1. Is buttery and rich, with a very slight acidity
2. Has character and communicates a sense of place (terroir)

E. Flow/melt
1. Cheese melts and flows fully and completely rather than remaining a cohesive, tense mass

	SAMPLE 1	SAMPLE 2	SAMPLE 3	SAMPLE 4	SAMPLE 5	SAMPLE 6	SAMPLE 7
A. Color							
B. Tolerance							
C. Texture							
D. Character							
E. Flow							
Total							
Average							

Add up the numbers in each column and divide by 5. The sample with the highest number is the one you should use.

Notes: _____   _____   _____

_____   _____   _____

_____   _____   _____

PART 2
TECHNIQUES

Before you measure a single gram of flour, spend some time getting familiar with the techniques of dough making. Each and every step in the process, from mixing and bulk fermenting to shaping and baking, leaves its own impact on the final product. No single step is more important or less deserving of mastery than another. Each plays a fundamental role in achieving the ideal pizza. Understanding what each of these stages does individually is hugely important to pizza success.

Mixing the dough incorporates the ingredients and ensures they are distributed evenly, which is essential for efficient fermentation. Handling the dough in a way that builds strength—I call these movements "stretch and folds"—is critical for developing gluten, which traps gas in the dough as it rises. Shaping portions of the dough sets the structure for your pizza. Careful handling maintains the fermented dough's protein network. Stretching elongates the dough and readies it to receive toppings. Baking brings all your work together and turns your dough into crust. The next step is the best part: tasting. (Scan the QR codes throughout the chapter to see techniques in action.)

The first set of instructions is for making round pies; instructions for pan pizzas follow. The techniques are similar for both round pizzas and pan pies. Dough for a round pie weighs 200 to 275 grams (depending on the diameter and oven of choice) and bakes directly in a home oven at 500°F for 6 to 7 minutes, or in a high temperature oven for a shorter duration. Dough for a pan pie weighs 850 to 900 grams and bakes in a steel pan at 475°F for 22 minutes. You can bake a round pie in a wood fired or high temperature oven but not a pan pie. The dough for pan pies performs best at consistent lower temperatures.

In both cases, I approach making the dough for the pizza by naming my intention: I want to bake an exceptional pizza with a nice open crumb, a firm, crisp, fully brown undercarriage, a caramelized rim, uniform oven spring, and properly cooked toppings. I include even more specific intentions related to every step in a dedicated box at the beginning of each section. I also keep the Pizza Evaluation Rubric (page xviii) in mind with each step. After close to two decades of experimenting, I have found that mixing, fermenting, shaping, stretching, launching, and baking my dough as I have laid out in this section is the way to get there.

Once you've joined me on my journey to my ideal pizza, I want you to decide what exceptional pizza is to you. The Pizza Evaluation Rubric hits all of the characteristics that I love about pizza, but if your preferences lie elsewhere, you can modify my recipes and methods to suit you.

BEFORE YOU START

I know how tempting it is to want to jump in and start baking pizzas, but I suggest spending some time familiarizing yourself with the techniques and accompanying videos before getting started. It's a lot easier to flip through this book and watch videos on your smartphone without having dough on your hands!

Before you even start mixing, gather all the ingredients you'll need to mix the dough: flour, water, salt, and your chosen leavening agent. You'll also need a probe thermometer, metric scales, a large bowl, plastic wrap, and clean kitchen towels. Grab a spoon if you want to use it to mix, but totally feel free to use your hands—I do!

CALCULATE TARGET WATER TEMPERATURE

NAME YOUR INTENTION:
Manage the temperature of your ingredients so the dough begins fermentation at the same temperature every time for consistent results.

The key to successful baking, whether it's pizza or bread, lies in managing variables. Any time we can isolate a variable, like temperature, and control it, we will end up with better results. If dough starts fermenting at different temperatures each day, you lose some control over the fermentation process. Fermentation occurs faster at warmer temperatures and progresses more slowly at cooler temperatures. If you can keep the temperature of the mixed dough constant every time you mix, you will ensure that it is always fermenting at the same rate, therefore creating more predictable results. If you don't ferment your dough under the same conditions each time, you can't look back on your previous results to make corrections.

Each dough recipe in Part 3 specifies a desired dough temperature (DDT), 73 to 78°F. That is the ideal temperature for the dough to reach after mixing. To achieve the stated DDT, measure the air temperature, flour temperature, the temperature of the starter, if using, and the temperature generated by friction when mixing (Friction Factor, page 73).

The Friction Factor is usually no more than 1 or 2°F when mixing by hand but could be 15 to 30°F or more with a spiral mixer, and around 40°F for a KitchenAid with a dough hook. Because the Friction Factor may be a significant amount of heat, it's important to take into consideration, especially when using a mechanical mixer.

I use a thermometer to measure each temperature in °F, then plug them into one of these equations:

Target water temperature formula for recipes using instant yeast:

(DDT x 3) − (Air Temperature + Flour Temperature + Friction Factor) = Target Water Temperature (°F)

Target water temperature formula for recipes using starter:

(DDT x 4) − (Air Temperature + Flour Temperature + Starter Temperature + Friction Factor) = Target Water Temperature (°F)

The resulting number gives you the temperature your water needs to be. If your ambient temperature or tap are on the warmer side, you may need to cool the water to the desired temperature with ice (remove the ice from the water; do not add it to the dough). If you're in a very hot place and the formula's results are a water temperature below freezing, refrigerate your flour to drop its temperature. Once the flour has cooled, measure its temperature again and plug it into the DDT equation to ascertain your new target water temperature. This is mainly going to be a factor in an extremely hot location in the summer and when using a mixer.

We apply the same concept to starter temperature when preparing the final feeding. Each recipe that includes starter states a desired starter temperature (DST). To calculate the temperature of the water you will need, use the following formula:

Target water temperature formula for final starter feeding:

(DST x 4) − (Air Temperature + Starter Temperature + Flour Temperature) = Target Water Temperature (°F)

I would be remiss if I didn't mention here that the calculation isn't the exact temperature because the equation does not take into consideration the relative weights of each ingredient, which would impact the final number. Weighted math is a lot more complex, so I am providing the above equation, which is accurate enough to give really good results.

WEIGH INGREDIENTS

Next, weigh out all of your ingredients. You'll need a metric scale that measures fractions of a gram (like the one a jeweler would use) if you're using commercial yeast and a standard gram scale. Both are inexpensive and essential tools for baking. If you are using a starter, make sure it is fully active before you intend to mix. For more information on building a starter, see page 155.

MIX THE DOUGH

NAME YOUR INTENTION
Bring the dough together so the ingredients are distributed evenly, begin to develop gluten.

I often joke that I mix by hand at home because there's no room for a mixer on my kitchen counter and anyway I'm too lazy to wash it. There's more to it than that, of course. I absolutely love getting my hands in the dough. It puts me in close contact, providing me with crucial information about the dough's gluten development (strength, elasticity, and extensibility), gas production, and hydration (see next page). There's also no greater joy in my life than mixing dough by hand with my young daughter, then washing her hands over the sink after she has mixed and kneaded.

When mixing by hand, bits of dough will stick to your hands. It's hard to wash them off with soap and water. I use vinegar, which breaks down the dough, as a more efficient cleanser. As any baker who has worked with acidic starter way past its prime will know, acid breaks down gluten.

Over the years, I have mixed so many doughs that I can discern even small variations in my dough's characteristics simply by feeling it with my hands. Direct contact with my dough has made me a better baker and it will absolutely make you one, too. It's just not practical to hand mix dough for 500 pizzas for weekend service, so at Razza, we use a mechanical mixer. But if I could get away with a hand mix, I would!

Mixing involves several stages of dough making:

- The first step is incorporating the ingredients, the stage in which you combine the flour, water, and instant yeast if using. If you are mixing dough made with starter, do not add the starter until after the flour and water have rested together.

- Autolyse, or allowing flour and water to rest together for 20 minutes to 1 hour, hydrates the flour before you add the other ingredients.

- Incorporating the starter (if using) and salt comes next. When I bake with sourdough starter, I add it after the autolyse.

- Finally, mixing to the desired stage of dough development prepares the dough for the next stage of dough making, Bulk Ferment with Stretch and Folds (page 77).

Hydration

Hydration occurs when you add water to flour, activating the flour's enzymes and engaging the starches and proteins. You can observe how the flour and water interact when mixed: The water is absorbed by the flour to form a shaggy dough. Over time, the dough changes, becomes more cohesive, more elastic, and more extensible. These characteristics develop due to what is happening in the mixture on a molecular level.

Water molecules flood the starch and protein molecules of the flour, changing their structure and allowing compounds to flow and interact more freely. The water bonds with the flour's proteins, glutenin and gliadin, to form gluten and allows the gluten to bond to more gluten, forming a 3D matrix of protein chains—imagine thousands of linked and interwoven rubber bands. These chains increase in length and complexity through kneading. The relative elasticity of these gluten chains, along with the other microscopic reactions within the dough, enables the dough to trap bubbles of carbon dioxide gas within it and to expand when the leavening agent ferments the dough.

Hydration also activates enzymes in the flour such as amylase and protease. Amylase is an essential enzyme present in flour. It is activated when flour is hydrated, and it converts the flour's starches (complex carbohydrates) into simpler compounds (simple sugars) that the yeast feeds on. As the yeast digests the simple sugars, it produces carbon dioxide, heat, and alcohol. I elaborate more on this stage in the fermentation section on page 80.

Protease is an enzyme that "cuts" proteins such as gluten. A small amount of protease activity creates a supple dough, but too much will break down the gluten and degrade the dough. Mills test for protease to ensure the flour they sell is not too rich in this enzyme.

Hydration and Oven Temperature

The doughs in this book have relatively high hydration. Dough hydration needs to match your oven for good results. High hydration dough is adapted to cooking at comparatively lower temperatures (like 500°F in a home oven) for longer periods of time, while ovens that get hotter than 600°F (such as wood fired ovens) cook the dough more quickly and should have lower hydration to get the same results. Water aids heat transfer so in a low temperature oven a higher hydration dough contributes to more efficient browning and creates a more even bake. A high hydration dough baked in a high temperature oven would burn, as the elevated quantity of water would transfer heat too efficiently.

When you first load the dough into the oven, the yeast continues to be active, releasing carbon dioxide, which causes the gas pockets in the gluten network to further expand. The water in the dough is also heated. The water that is trapped in the dough's gluten structure is partially converted to steam, while the moisture on the exterior of the dough evaporates and causes the outer layer to dry out. Meanwhile, the dough's proteins coagulate and harden. My dough was developed so that when these two events occur in the oven in unison, the result is a thin, eggshell crust. In order to get that result every time, be sure to let your oven recover between bakes so the dough is always subjected to the same heat.

The name of the game when it comes time to create your own dough recipes is to find that sweet spot in which the flour is hydrated sufficiently and there is the ideal hydration to produce the desired outcome based on your intentions.

Double Hydration

Double hydration means adding water in two separate phases of mixing, before gluten is developed and after. Typically, I use the double hydration technique when I am using a mixer. Gluten develops faster and more efficiently at a lower hydration. If you're making a 70 percent hydration dough, which is relatively high, to reduce the mixing time, hold back 15 percent of the water in the initial mix (so if your recipe calls for 500 grams of water, use 425 grams), and mix the dough until it is smooth and has reached medium gluten development (see page 74), then add the remaining 75 grams of water slowly. Once all the water has been incorporated, your mix is finished.

I also use the double hydration technique if I am using a freshly milled or high extraction flour, or generally a flour I have never worked with before and am not sure how it will absorb water. By adding the water in two phases, you can use your senses to determine when the flour is properly hydrated, rather than following a recipe that may call for more water than the flour can hold. The "Choose Your Own Adventure" Dough (page 163) uses this technique.

INCORPORATE INGREDIENTS

NAME YOUR INTENTION

Hydrate the flour and yeast, evenly disperse the yeast (if using), initiate enzymatic activity.

During this stage, you are not manipulating the dough intensely or for an extended length of time. You are mainly interested in ensuring the flour, water, and commercial yeast (if the recipe calls for it) are combined and hydrated. Be sure to mix the flour and instant yeast together first before you add the water to ensure the yeast is evenly dispersed in the dough. Add the water and mix with your hands or a spoon. Use a bowl that is large enough to incorporate all the ingredients without spilling. For the recipes in this book I recommend a large bowl.

AUTOLYSE (NATURALLY LEAVENED DOUGH)/RESTING PERIOD (YEASTED DOUGH)

NAME YOUR INTENTION
Fully hydrate the flour, begin gluten development, give enzymatic reactions a head start.

In baking terms, the period during which a mixture of flour and water rests together before the other ingredients are introduced is called autolyse. This step hydrates the flour (and therefore its proteins and starches), initiates gluten development, and allows the enzymes present in the flour time to do their work before their activity is slowed by the addition of salt. During this period, the starch begins to break down into simpler sugars that the yeast will consume as it ferments the dough. Autolyse reduces the amount of time you need to mix later and should last for a minimum of 20 minutes (but 1 hour or more is ideal).

Every time I water plants I think about autolyse and dough development. You can water a plant by dumping a bucket of water on it—and have the water mostly run off, without being absorbed. Or you could mimic nature and apply a slow drip like rain water, which hydrates the soil slowly in a way that benefits the plant. Flour particles are very small and need time to soak up the water and fully hydrate before the fermentation process begins.

The naturally leavened dough recipes in Part 3 call for a strict autolyse (flour and water alone), while the yeasted doughs introduce commercial yeast in this step. While the latter is not technically an autolyse (in fact, let's call it the resting period), the yeasted dough recipes allow flour, water, and commercial yeast to rest together, which gives the benefits of autolyse with the added feature of activating the yeast. It allows the yeast to be evenly dispersed in the dough, too. I always do a resting period when I bake with instant yeast.

Weigh starter, if using.

Add starter to autolysed dough.

Sprinkle salt over the d

Use the Rubaud method to fully incorporate stater.

INCORPORATE THE STARTER AND SALT

NAME YOUR INTENTION

Disperse the starter, if using, and salt evenly through the dough to ensure consistent fermentation.

When I add starter to the autolysed dough, I mix it in using the Rubaud method (see next page for images): I secure the bowl with my nondominant hand. Using four closed fingers, pinky to index, I scoop my hand under the far end of the dough, lift slightly, drop, and scoop again. I repeat the scooping/digging motion, turning the bowl slightly every four or five scoops, until the starter is completely incorporated. Then I sprinkle over the salt, scissor pinching it into the dough using my thumb and first finger to work it in from one side to the next until it is evenly incorporated and dissolved.

SCISSOR PINCH METHOD

SCAN FOR VIDEO

Scissor pinch the salt into the dough.

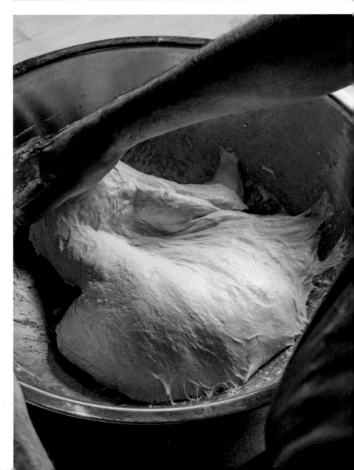

KNEAD

Once all ingredients have been incorporated, I mix to medium gluten development —the dough will show signs of elasticity but you won't be able to pass the Window Pane Test (see page 75). My approach is to knead the ingredients together using the Rubaud method until fully incorporated, then continue kneading for 5 to 7 minutes more to build some initial strength in the dough. You will feel the dough begin to tighten up and become stronger under your fingertips. I follow this stage with a long bulk fermentation. Both stages are related to the dough's ability to hold together, its ability to be stretched and pulled without tearing, and its capacity to trap gases as it rises. I build strength (and flavor!) over time during bulk fermentation by doing stretch and folds at regular intervals.

When you think you're done mixing, use the Window Pane Test to assess the dough's level of gluten development.

Friction Factor

Friction Factor is the quantity of heat generated by mixing that is transferred to the dough. While hand mixing generates a small quantity of heat, barely 1 or 2°F, a spiral mixer or KitchenAid with a dough hook may generate up to 40°F. That's a lot of heat! To determine the Friction Factor of your mixer for a specific batch size for the first time, mix the dough, then take the dough's final temperature. Subtract the desired dough temperature (see page 62) from the actual dough temperature, and the resulting figure is the Friction Factor for that mixer and that batch size. You'll need to use that number in the desired dough temperature equation to ascertain the water temperature you need when initially mixing the dough.

Professional and Home Mixers

If you have a stand mixer or spiral mixer at home, that's great. I have a couple and, while I prefer hand mixing, I will pull out my spiral mixer if I'm whipping up a triple batch or more of dough. For anything smaller, it's so easy to use a bowl and mix the dough by hand. I always mix small batches by hand and I suggest you do, too.

If, instead, you prefer to use a mixer, bear in mind that the machine can build a lot of strength in the dough—we get this with hand mixed dough by doing stretch and folds at intervals during bulk fermentation. If you are using a mechanical mixer, you have the opportunity to shorten the bulk fermentation time because a lot of that strength-building work is being done in the mixer. For My Everyday Dough (page 146), for example, you can reduce the stretch and folds to one time only if using a mixer, provided the dough passes the Window Pane Test.

Be conscious of the stage of dough development you bring the dough to in the mixer and aim for medium gluten development (see page 74). Mixers have the possibility of taking you past the stage of medium gluten development if you get carried away. Monitor the dough closely. If you go too far, mixing to full gluten development in the mixer, you should limit the bulk fermentation time to 30 minutes to 1 hour. This scenario isn't ideal because it doesn't contribute to building flavor, which is best developed over time.

A mixer introduces heat into the mixing process, which you have to take into account. Mechanical mixers also incorporate oxygen into the dough. If you mix too long, you could introduce too much of it, having negative impacts on the dough's flavor and color.

Mixing and Gluten Development

Dough develops gluten in stages as the dough is mixed and fermented. The short or gentle mix basically brings the flour, water, salt, and leavening agent (commercial yeast or preferment) together. The mixture will be very sticky at this stage and will pull apart easily because the gluten development hasn't begun in any significant way. A dough that is subjected only to a short mix will require a very long bulk fermentation period with multiple stretch and folds performed at intervals in order to achieve full gluten development.

If you use a mixer, as I do at Razza, gluten further develops through mixing, creating the moderately strong network that will trap gases in the dough as it ferments and rises. This is the improved mix, which renders the dough tacky but not sticky, ensures the ingredients are distributed evenly, and incorporates a small amount of oxygen. Once the dough is mixed, I set

it aside and begin a series of stretch and folds at intervals, which, in addition to time, brings the dough to full gluten development. You know your dough has reached full gluten development when it passes the Window Pane Test (opposite).

The intensive mix applies to commercial and industrial bakers using mechanical mixers. Driven by economic and time constraints, this approach favors building strength and full gluten development quickly in a mixer, rather than through a long bulk fermentation. The dough is kneaded vigorously, building a tremendous amount of strength and fully developing the gluten. This phase also introduces excessive oxygen to the dough, which may oxidize it, causing it to lose color and flavor. I avoid this step when using a mixer so my dough doesn't develop too much strength, which reduces bulk fermentation time at the expense of flavor.

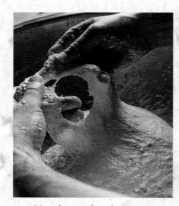
No gluten development

Medium gluten development

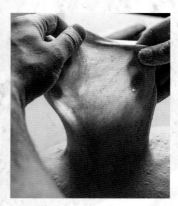
Full gluten development

The small air pockets created in the dough during the mix are called nucleation sites. Think of them as tiny bubbles ready to receive carbon dioxide gases as the dough ferments and, later, steam as the dough bakes.

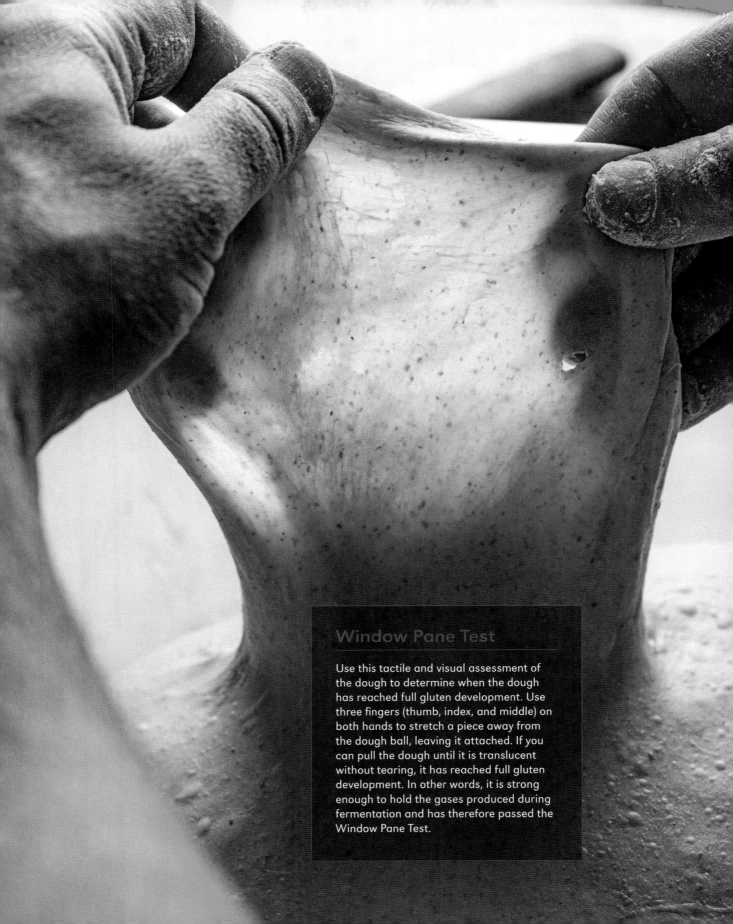

Window Pane Test

Use this tactile and visual assessment of the dough to determine when the dough has reached full gluten development. Use three fingers (thumb, index, and middle) on both hands to stretch a piece away from the dough ball, leaving it attached. If you can pull the dough until it is translucent without tearing, it has reached full gluten development. In other words, it is strong enough to hold the gases produced during fermentation and has therefore passed the Window Pane Test.

BULK FERMENT WITH STRETCH AND FOLDS

NAME YOUR INTENTION
Build strength and bring the dough to full gluten development, develop flavor, manage fermentation so the dough increases in volume, equalize the dough temperature, redistribute gases.

After kneading, I transfer the dough to an oiled bowl, cover it, and set it aside. This marks the beginning of bulk fermentation. I like to use a clear container so I can observe the level of activity and see any bubbles forming as the dough bulk ferments. The container should be large enough to accommodate the dough rising with room to spare.

Bulk fermentation is also known as primary or first fermentation (the secondary fermentation, or proofing stage, comes after the dough is divided and rounded into balls; see page 88). During this first phase, there is potentially a lot of flavor development, gluten development is progressing, and gases are being trapped in the dough's gluten network as it ferments. Bulk fermentation is complete when there is gas production and full gluten development. In other words, the dough has increased in volume by 20 to 25 percent and it passes the Window Pane Test (see page 75).

Stretch and folds done at intervals during bulk fermentation build strength and tension, equalize the dough temperature so it all ferments at the same rate, and redistribute gases. Fold with wet hands (my preference; you can use very lightly oiled, too, but never mix oil with water at this stage), so the dough doesn't stick to your fingers. You will actually feel the dough tighten up as you work with it. The duration of bulk fermentation depends on your kitchen temperature (it goes more quickly the warmer the room is), how fast the fermentation is moving, and how much gluten was developed during mixing, but typically if you do stretch and folds every 30 minutes, the dough may reach this point within 2 to 4 hours. Always do the Window Pane Test before each series of stretch and folds to determine the status of the dough's gluten development.

There are several approaches to stretch and folds. I like the envelope fold. Starting at 12 o'clock, I pull the quadrant of dough upward gently 6 to 12 inches (as much as the dough allows without tearing), then press it gently onto itself. Then I turn the bowl a half turn and repeat. Next, I turn the bowl a quarter turn and repeat the lifting/pressing, then a half turn and repeat. I then set the dough aside, covered with plastic wrap or a clean kitchen towel, at room temperature for another 30 minutes. Another stretch and fold technique is the coil fold.

ENVELOPE FOLD

COIL FOLD

Envelope Fold

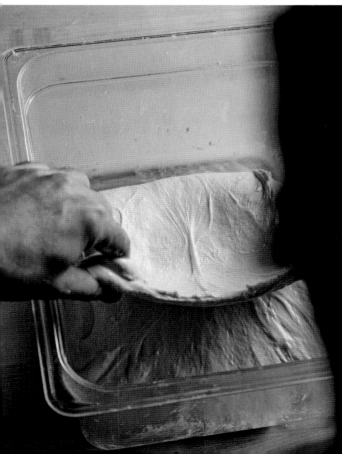

FERMENTATION

NAME YOUR INTENTION
Build flavor over time through fermentation, manage the fermentation temperature for consistent results, ferment the dough properly so the final product fulfills the Pizza Evaluation Rubric's standards (caramelization, oven spring, etc.).

Fermentation is a function of time, temperature, and quantity of inoculation (the concentration of yeast in the dough). The recipes and formulas in this book will help you bake with commercial yeast or starter reliably by controlling the temperature of fermentation, both for your dough, as well as your starter (if using), contributing to reliable, successful results.

Commercial yeast and the yeasts present in the starter consume the simple sugars in the dough and convert them into carbon dioxide, which gets trapped in the gluten network, causing the dough to rise. Alcohol and heat are other byproducts of fermentation. The alcohol evaporates when the dough is baked. Bacteria present in the starter, meanwhile, consume sugars and convert them to lactic acid (the one that curdles dairy in yogurt and cheese) and acetic acid (the same acid present in vinegar). These give naturally fermented doughs their slightly sour flavors (I prefer gentle acidity as opposed to notably sour doughs). Notes of acetic acid are not desirable because they make your final product taste vinegary. The lactic acid is gentler and brings notes to your dough that are more floral and complex.

A key to making dough with a starter is to keep the acids and yeasts in balance by using the starter at the right time in its life cycle (see page 156) before the acids proliferate too intensely. Maintaining the acid-yeast balance ensures the dough will ferment properly, rise correctly, and taste complex but not overly acidic. Doing so requires feeding the starter on a regular schedule and using the starter to make dough when it is at or before its peak of activity.

Making bread or pizza with a starter may seem challenging but it's really not. If you practice it consistently, it gets easier every time. You wouldn't build a garden to grow one tomato. You plant your garden to reap a more abundant harvest each year, building on lessons learned the previous season. That's how I see sourdough baking. It requires feeding and maintenance, but if you're anything like me, tending it will bring you closer to your baking practice—and give you the joy of nurturing something every day. As you bake with it, you will gain a deeper understanding of how your yeast and bacteria colonies work and where your starter is in its life cycle at a given time. It's taken years of observing my starter to gain a fuller understanding of how to harness its potential, but the rewards have been many. Like a gardener tending a field, I have nurtured my starter and reaped the benefits of being engaged with this living thing over many years. It's almost like part of my family.

12 pm
80°

SHAPE AND PROOF

NAME YOUR INTENTION

Set the size of the dough ball, which will impact the pizza dimensions, set the structure of the pizza, redistribute gases, strengthen the gluten network, create tension in the dough for the purpose of promoting oven spring, and aid stretching the dough effectively.

Once bulk fermentation is complete, you have a fairly delicate dough on your hands. Handle it gently as you prepare it for its final fermentation phase, so the baked pizza texture is light and airy.

DIVIDE AND ROUND (PRE-SHAPE)

Once bulk fermentation is complete, it's time to divide and round the dough, splitting the dough into individual dough balls for round or pan pies. Be as gentle as possible and don't overhandle the dough so you do not crush the bubbles the yeast produced during bulk fermentation.

Flour the top of the dough, then turn it out onto a smooth, clean, lightly floured surface. Allow the dough to release from the bowl as gently as possible. Once bulk fermentation is complete, any pressure that is exerted on the dough will affect the texture of the final product. The gases should remain as evenly distributed as possible. It's impossible to totally eliminate damage, but you want to limit it. If the dough sticks to your fingers, dip your clean, dry fingers in flour before touching it again. I keep a little bowl next to the work surface for this purpose.

Once you have turned the dough out from the bowl, keep track of the "top" and "bottom." Doing so will contribute to better oven spring and respect the tension created during the rounding phase when you bake the pizza. The top of the future pizza is the part of the turned-out dough that is touching the countertop. Use a bench scraper to divide the dough into pieces (the size will depend on whether you are making round or pan pies), transferring each piece of dough to a lightly floured scale to ensure consistency. Cut from one corner of the dough mass. While dividing, touch the dough as little as possible. Be gentle with it but use decisive movements to slice the dough and transfer it to the scale, keeping the part that was touching the counter on the surface of the scale. Cut off any excess directly from the ball on the scale. Place excess aside. If the dough portion is too light, cut a piece from the excess or the dough mass and attach to the top of the dough piece.

Every time you cut into the dough you're disturbing the network of gluten. We want the balls to be the exact same size but we want to minimize the cuts. You'll get better at eyeballing the weight the more you practice so you will end up touching the dough less.

Once weighed, transfer each piece of dough to a lightly floured, clean, and very dry place next to the scale. The part that touched the scale should rest on the counter. Once you have weighed out all the dough, begin pre-shaping, forming the dough into round balls that will become your individual pizzas.

Pre-shaping the dough builds tension and strength, redistributes gases, sets the structure, and prepares the dough for shaping into round pizzas. This step is similar to what you did during the stretch and folds, but on a smaller scale. This is the stage during which you will feel how strong the dough is based on how many movements it takes to tighten up, and therefore where the dough falls on the elasticity/extensibility continuum.

I take my cues from the bread world and keep the dough on the table while pre-shaping, using the tension of the dough against the surface to tighten and shape the ball, instead of lifting it and manipulating it with my fingers as many pizza makers do. The first step is to bring the top half of the dough (from 12 o'clock) and lift and press it into the center of the dough. Next, bring the bottom half of the dough and lift and press it into the center. Then, take the left side of the dough and lift and press it into the center. Repeat with the right side. Then, take the four corners and pull and fold them into the center of the ball and gently press to attach. Do not flatten. Keep track of the "top" and "bottom" of the dough as it relates to your future pizza. Be sure the ball is round and the bottom is sealed, pinching it closed if necessary, before setting it aside, seam-side down.

Throughout the pre-shaping process, take care to incorporate as little flour as possible, brushing off any excess as needed. You want to use a bit of flour to prevent sticking without adding loads of dry flour to your dough.

DIVIDE AND
ROUND

SCAN FOR VIDEO

Freezing the Dough

I don't fully endorse freezing dough, but it can be done, albeit with less enticing results than following the dough schedules laid out in the recipes. If you want to freeze the dough, you can do so after it is divided and rounded. Place it in a sealed container for up to a month, then defrost overnight in your refrigerator. Bring the dough to room temperature, then set aside until the dough passes the Poke Test (page 89), indicating it is ready to bake.

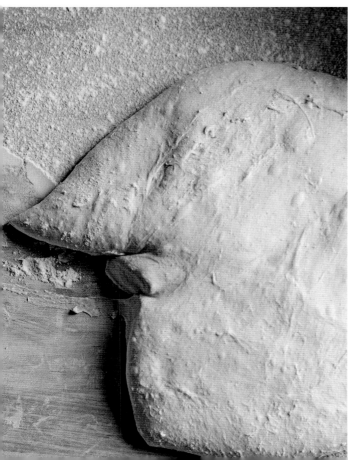

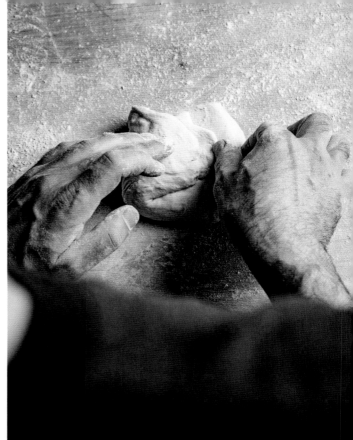

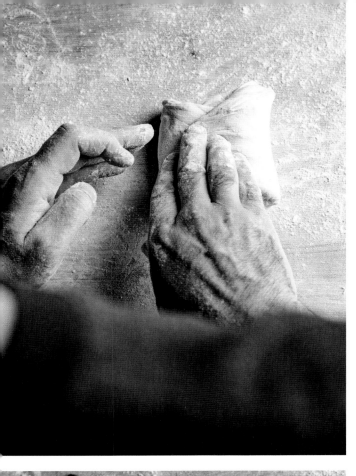
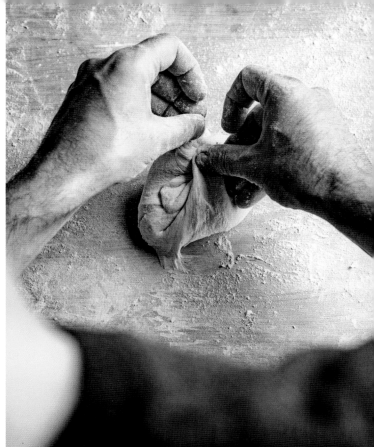

PROOF

To store the dough for secondary fermentation (proofing), use containers with enough room to allow the dough to at least double in size as it continues to rise. You can use very lightly oiled deli pint containers (for round pies) or larger takeout containers (for pan pies) with lids or a floured quarter- or half-sheet pan (in this case be sure to dust the dough balls with flour before covering with plastic wrap). I use floured DoughMate artisan dough trays with lids, which I love because they fit in a home refrigerator and are designed for serious home pizza makers.

For dough made with commercial yeast, transfer it to the refrigerator to ferment overnight (or for at least 12 hours). For dough made with starter, you have a choice at this stage. You can either set the dough aside at room temperature for a few hours and bake it off that day, or you can refrigerate it overnight to develop even more flavor.

Refrigerator temperatures are very cool, averaging 38°F, which significantly slows the fermentation; keep your compressor clean to ensure it is working properly and always cooling to the desired temperature. If you put the dough in the back near the blower it's potentially going to be colder compared to the front. Your refrigerator temperature will also be affected by how frequently you open it. Lately I have been using my small wine refrigerator set to 52°F for the cold fermentation phase and the results have been great. The yeast is more active at that higher temperature and the dough ferments at a nice pace, producing wonderful aromas. If you don't have such a fridge but do have a balcony or backyard where you can store your dough overnight, use that instead (only if the temperature falls in the 50 to 60°F range).

One of the many joyful things about fermentation is getting creative, learning about your environment, and experimenting with ways to adapt to it for great results. Yeast is a living thing and it responds to environmental factors in a really discernible way. The more you bake and learn the nuances of your microclimate, the more intuitive you will become as a baker.

BRING THE DOUGH TO ROOM TEMPERATURE

Remove the dough from the refrigerator. The dough should have increased in volume by at least 20 percent. Allow it to reach room temperature before you bake. Based on your refrigerator and kitchen temperature, it may take 2 to 3 hours for the dough to reach room temperature. Be patient. You don't want to put cold or lethargic dough into the oven for a number of reasons. If you bake cold dough, the crust won't rise properly, you won't get as much oven spring, the crust browning will be lackluster, the crust will be dense, and it will take longer to bake so your sauce may over-reduce and your cheese may break. Everything you have done thus far is leading up to this, so you want the dough to perform at its max. Keep in mind that a wood fired oven takes hours to preheat so take your dough out accordingly.

The dough ball is ready to stretch when it has reached room temperature, has increased in volume by another 20 percent, and passes the Poke Test (opposite). Once the dough reaches this point, the amount of time that the dough remains in this optimal state and is in its prime depends on an array of factors: your room temperature, if you mixed and fermented at the proper dough temperature, the temperature of your refrigerator, and how many times you opened the door while the dough was fermenting, to name a few. Ideally it will remain in its prime for a few hours, but you won't know until you start baking with it.

Poke Test

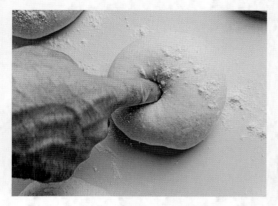

To determine if your dough is ready to bake with, poke it with a floured index finger. If it springs back slowly and leaves a slight indentation when poked, it's ready. If it springs back quickly and leaves no indentation, it's not ready yet. If your finger leaves an impression or causes the dough to collapse, it has overproofed.

Failed Poke Test

Passed Poke Test

PREHEAT YOUR OVEN

At least 1 hour before baking, preheat the oven to 500°F and set a baking stone or steel on a rack 6 to 8 inches below the top of the oven to preheat as well. You want your oven as hot as possible, so turn the broiler on during the last 10 minutes if your oven allows. Turn off the broiler before you load the oven.

If baking in a wood fired oven, follow the instructions starting on page 123. Preheat your high temperature oven according to the user manual.

Use this time to prepare your toppings, grab some rice flour, and gather your tools for baking.

STRETCH AND BUILD

PREPARE TO STRETCH

NAME YOUR INTENTION

Elongate the dough in a gentle manner and stretch to uniform thickness in order to aid the texture of the final product and provide a structurally sound base for your toppings.

> High hydration doughs risk sticking to the peel if they rest there too long. Be sure to have all your toppings prepared well before you stretch so you're not scrambling as you build your round pie.

While the dough reaches room temperature, prepare a clean, dry work area. Select and prepare your toppings, allowing time for them to reach room temperature. (If you put cold cheese or sauce on a pizza, the oven will have to work harder to heat them.) Bear in mind that some toppings, like Fermented Chili Sauce (page 248), require preparation several days in advance.

You want an ample workspace that will accommodate the dough and toppings. For me, that means at least 3 by 3 feet, but the bigger the space, the more comfortable your shaping process will be.

Flour the top of a dough ball. If it is in a container, turn the dough out onto a generously floured surface. If it is in a dough tray or resting on a baking sheet, with your nondominant hand resting gently on top of the floured dough ball, use a dough scraper to scoop up the dough. Then invert it and gently land it on the floured surface. Try not to damage any of the structure, and be as minimally invasive as possible. Keep track of the "top" and "bottom" of the dough. The top of your future pizza is the one currently resting on the countertop.

Alternatively, transfer the dough to a heavily floured rimmed baking sheet. This will contain the flour in one place, facilitating cleanup.

STRETCH (SHAPE) A ROUND PIZZA

Stretching, building, and baking instructions for the Pan Pie begin on page 117.

This step is one of the most exciting. After you've developed the dough, it is finally ready to be shaped into a pizza. Take note of how the dough feels beneath your fingertips, how hydrated it feels, and how extensible and elastic it is. Using extremely gentle movements with flat fingertips spread, apply pressure on the dough at 10 and 2 o'clock. Lift your hands and reposition them on the dough closer to you. Move from the top of the dough toward you, pressing downward and outward. Leave an inch along the rim that you don't touch at all. This untouched area will become the crusty rim. Pressing on it at this stage will result in a compromised crust. You should reach the bottom edge of the dough in about four movements. If the dough sticks to your fingers or the work surface, dust it with a bit more flour. Err on the side of using more flour, not less. You'll shake off any excess before it goes on the peel.

Flip the dough over. The top of the future pizza is now facing upward. Continue stretching the dough, using the technique that works best for you. One approach is to leave the dough on the counter and, with one hand in the center, pull at 3, 6, 9, and 12 o'clock. Another is to scoop up the dough from below with your palms facing the counter, then turn the dough, stretching and pulling it in increments with your knuckles. Be super gentle and don't be afraid to rely on gravity, a great stretcher of pizza dough. Regardless of your technique, stretch the dough until you get to a 10- to 11-inch diameter. You will stretch it to a 12-inch diameter on the peel.

**STRETCH A
ROUND PIZZA**

SCAN FOR VIDEO

Calzone Rescue

Okay, so you got a little excited while stretching the dough and tore a hole in it. Pinching the hole closed is a risky remedy. When this happens to me, I just make a calzone out of it, folding over half the dough and pinching it closed around the toppings. It might not be what I intended to make, but it is delicious!

Stretching on the counter.

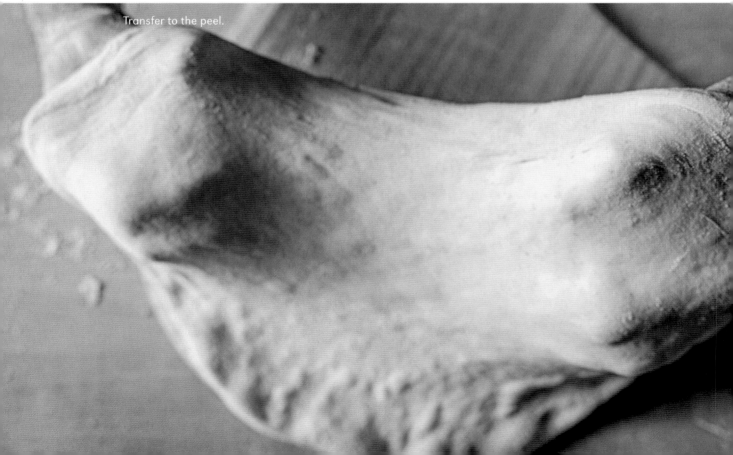

Transfer to the peel.

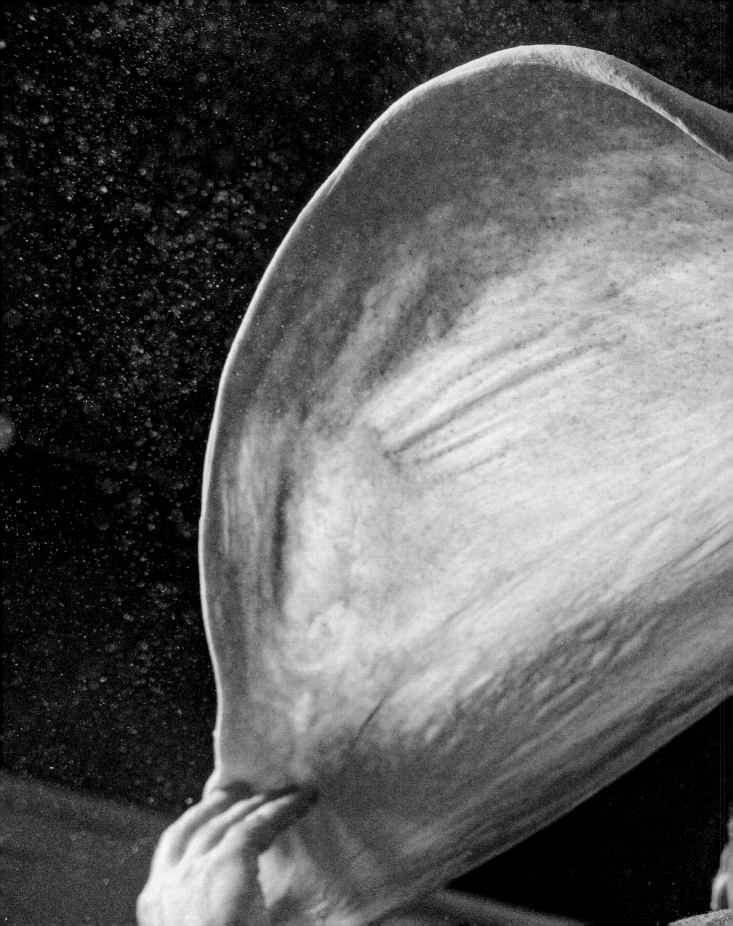

PAUSE AND ASSESS

If you're using the dough at the right time in its life cycle, it should open very easily. This is a moment when you can stop and reflect on the dough and note any necessary adjustments for your next batch. If the dough snaps back, you may have waited too long during bulk fermentation to pre-shape it. If it tears, you may not have developed enough strength during bulk fermentation, the dough may have overfermented, or you may have used too much pressure to stretch. You can correct these flaws the next time (but in the meantime you should be able to stretch the dough if you are very gentle). That's why taking notes on your process is so important.

TRANSFER TO THE PEEL

Dust the peel with coarse rice flour, semolina, or cornmeal. I prefer rice flour because it falls away from the dough very easily, is the perfect color, and does not stick if it absorbs moisture.

Next, wipe your hands to remove any excess moisture. This final step of transferring the dough to the peel is a critical and awesome moment. Gently scoop up the dough, sliding your hands beneath it, palms facing the work surface. Note how it feels. If there is any moisture, return it to the floured surface momentarily, then proceed. Shake off any excess flour and transfer the dough to the floured peel. Using your fingertips, palms facing upward from underneath, gently pull the dough until the disk reaches 12 inches in diameter. Be sure your hands are dry when you do this, otherwise the dough will stick to the peel.

**TRANSFER PIZZA
TO A PEEL**

SCAN FOR VIDEO

BUILD

Building the ideal pizza is all about restraint. Keep it simple while taking into consideration the judgement criteria from the Pizza Evaluation Rubric (page xviii), like the dimensions of the pizza, the cheese-to-sauce ratio, and even distribution of toppings. See the recipes in Part 4 (page 169) for instructions for topping your pizza.

If your dough is very elastic, it can spring back to 10 inches, even with toppings weighing it down. If necessary, use your fingertips, palms facing upward from underneath, and gently pull the dough until it reaches 12 inches in diameter once again. Be sure not to disrupt the toppings and that your hands are dry when you do this, otherwise the dough will stick to the peel.

Be Gentle

Because the dough hydration is so high, the gluten is delicate and you need to be gentle with it. When you see NYC-style pizza makers hitting that dough really hard it's because they can. They use much stronger flour with more protein and lower hydration—and the result is a tougher, chewier crust. With the recipes in this book, we get relatively delicate doughs with 11 to 13 percent protein flour, so we want to manage the pressure we apply to them with our fingertips as we shape. It's one of the few moments that we have when we're actually touching the dough and you have an impact on the texture of that pizza. During most of this process you're not actually touching the dough. It's the mix, the folds, and getting it out of the container where you have to be deliberate and gentle. This is the moment when you can guarantee great texture or you can contribute to a flaw in the final product with too much touching. Great texture means a light, open, airy crumb. We spent so much time on the fermentation of this dough that you're still going to have delicious pizza—but if you overhandle the dough it will be a little bit more dense, and you won't have that eggshell crust and that super tender crumb.

BAKE

NAME YOUR INTENTION
Manage the bake time and oven temperature, bake until the crust demonstrates deep caramelization, bake until toppings are properly cooked.

I'm all about harnessing the heat of the broiler to get the oven and stone or steel even hotter. I start by preheating the oven for at least an hour, then turn on the broiler for 10 minutes before I load the pizza. The extra heat absorbed by the stone or steel translates into great oven spring and a sturdy, crisp, well browned undercarriage.

Clean the stone or steel between every few bakes, brushing it with a dry kitchen towel held with tongs, to prevent debris from sticking to the bottom of your pizza or burning in your oven.

PREPARE THE HOME OVEN

Many residential ovens max out at a high temperature of 500°F (not including the broiler) and that's just really not that hot in the grand scheme of baking. It's great for a high hydration pan pizza that's baked in a black pan for 22 minutes or a round pie baked on a stone or steel for 6 to 7 minutes. But you're not going to get the "leopard spots" on the rim that are so popular in wood fired pizza making, but are in fact a flaw. And that's okay. I don't want that effect. I'm after a sturdy product with even crust caramelization and a good crumb.

I can get the characteristics I love using the dough recipes in Part 3 and a familiarity with my home oven. Baking in an electric oven or a gas oven isn't as simple as turning the dial to the desired temperature. Ovens have hot spots and idiosyncrasies. Some take longer to recover between bakes than others. The way to get to know your oven is to use it.

To maximize oven spring and ensure you are harnessing the greatest potential of your oven, preheat the oven with a baking stone or steel placed on a rack 6 to 8 inches from the top of the oven. The stone or steel absorbs the oven's heat and transfers it to the dough.

The reason to use a stone or steel to bake on, and not just a thin metal pan, is their greater

---

Some home ovens reach 550°F. If yours can, set it to that temperature and bake as instructed here.

thermal mass. Thermal mass is the potential for a material to absorb and store heat. If you are baking in a wood fired oven (see page 123), you may have a hearth that is 6 inches thick and absorbs a lot of heat and takes a long time to heat up and cool down. In other words, its thermal mass is superior to that of a stone or steel in a home oven. The greater the thermal mass, the more efficiently the stone or steel will hold on to the heat, transfer it to the pizza, and contribute to oven spring and undercarriage caramelization.

At home, I use the Baking Steel developed by Andris Lagsdin, which is essentially a ¼-inch-thick steel plate. I bought my first one a few years ago and it's been in my oven ever since. It retains and transfers heat better than any home oven tool I have used. It makes my oven more efficient, too, because once it gets hot, it stays hot. Another trick I use to maximize thermal mass is to put fire bricks beneath my Baking Steel. I place them on a half-sheet pan so they are easy to move in and out of the oven, then rest the pan on a rack 6 to 8 inches from the top of the oven and place the Baking Steel on top of that. That way both the fire bricks and steel are absorbing and transferring heat.

Transferring a blast of heat to the pizza dough is essential for oven spring, crust browning, and caramelization. If you don't have enough heat built up, you're not going to have an adequate heat load to transfer to the food. Preheating the oven for at least an hour will give you the concentrated heat you need for a great final product.

If you don't have a baking stone or steel, you can use an inverted half-sheet pan, but it won't retain and transfer heat efficiently so I don't recommend it. In fact, you will end up with a blond (undercaramelized) undercarriage.

Oven Spring and Caramelization

Oven spring occurs when dough hits a hot surface, either a preheated stone or steel or a high temperature oven hearth, and a combination of rapid yeast activity and steam being generated from the dough's water content heating up causes it to puff up. The carbon dioxide from the yeast and the steam from the water inflate the bubbles in the gluten network, leading to a nice open crumb.

Once the pizza exhibits oven spring, begin to observe the rim of the pizza for signs of caramelization. Caramelization is the product of a complex series of chemical reactions, when the sugars in the dough brown as they are exposed to heat. The process occurs in stages, creating a spectrum of brown, red, and gray colors in the pizza crust, as well as the nutty and roasty flavors that accompany them. Caramelization is similar to the Maillard reaction, which is caused by the transformation of amino acids. The Maillard reaction also contributes to the coloring of the crust.

PERFECT OVEN SPRING

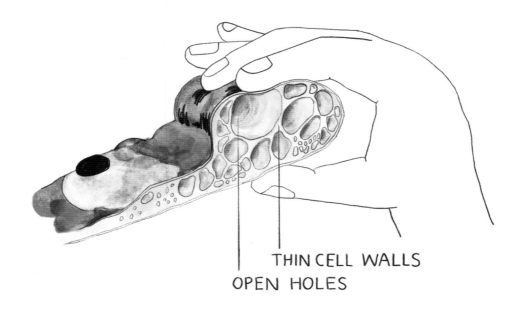

THIN CELL WALLS

OPEN HOLES

WHAT'S HAPPENING IN YOUR OVEN

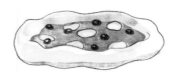

RAW PIZZA   OVEN SPRING   FULLY BAKED

BAKE

You've got your pizza on your peel. You topped it cautiously, making sure you didn't get any moisture onto the peel, and you've dried your hands. The oven is completely and fully preheated. Your whole house is hot. *It's time.*

Before you open the oven door, give the peel a quick jerk. The pizza should move slightly in response to your movements. If the pizza sticks to the peel, it's pretty hard to salvage. You can, theoretically, try to lift up the part of the dough that's stuck to the peel and dust it with additional rice flour, but for me it's not worth the risk of the dough staying stuck and launching cheese and sauce all over the inside of my oven. When this happens, I just fold the dough in half and make it into a calzone (see page 94), the most delicious way I know to recover from a round pizza failure.

There's a lot riding on this moment, but it's important to be confident as you launch the pizza into the oven. Swift, confident movements count. Grip the peel with your dominant hand and open the oven door with your other hand. Land the tip of the peel about a half inch from the far edge of the stone or steel. Pull the peel swiftly away,

cautiously allowing the dough to fall into place. Don't get discouraged if you don't pull this off at first. This is a legitimately difficult part of the process and it takes practice.

Close the door and turn on the oven light. The pizza needs to bake for 6 to 7 minutes. Set a timer for 3 minutes. Check the pizza at the 3-minute mark to inspect the oven spring and rim caramelization (see box on page 108). Oven spring should be complete—meaning the rim should be prominently raised. Caramelization should be in progress—meaning the rim will be beginning to brown. Most ovens have hot spots, so if you see one part is cooking more quickly than another, slide the peel underneath the pizza and use your fingers or tongs to reposition it so the pizza cooks evenly, then close the door quickly. You want all these movements to be efficient so the oven loses as little heat as possible. Set the timer for 3 minutes. The pizza should be baked and the toppings should be melted or cooked within 6 to 7 minutes total, but use your intuition to tell when the pizza is done.

LAUNCH PIZZA

SCAN FOR VIDEO

REST AND EVALUATE

Transfer the cooked pizza to a wire rack (rather than a tabletop or cutting board) to add any additional toppings. This lets steam escape and prevents moisture from collecting under the crust, which will dampen and soften the crust. Before adding the finishing ingredients, lift up the pizza and inspect the undercarriage for the correct level of caramelization (see below). If it's not quite caramelized enough, put it back into the oven for 30 seconds more. Inspect for and note any debris, burnt flour, or holes. The visual inspection of the undercarriage is my last moment to make that call of whether that pizza is truly cooked to perfection.

Next, add any finishing toppings with the pizza back on the rack, whether it's arugula, Parmigiano-Reggiano, and speck for the Montagna (page 207), Pecorino Romano for the Guancia (page 203), or basil and a drizzle of raw oil for the Margherita (page 174).

The pizza is almost ready to serve! The penultimate step is assessing it with the Pizza Evaluation Rubric (page xviii). I have my notebook at the ready so I don't waste any time and can enjoy the pizza as soon as possible. I examine what went right and assess how I can do better next time. No matter the outcome, even an imperfect pizza can be incredibly delicious. Especially when friends and family are around, the flaws fade away and nothing else matters but the act of enjoying the pizza together.

SLICE, EAT, AND ENJOY

Finally, transfer the pizza to a flat surface and slice it using whatever tool you have handy—scissors, a wheel, or a chef's knife all work well—and taste it!

Troubleshooting

As you evaluate your pizza, take notes on its positive and negative attributes so you can improve on the next batch.

- If the crust lacks complexity and flavor, the dough may have under fermented.

- If there's no oven spring, the dough is probably over or under fermented, the temperature of the oven wasn't hot enough, or you didn't develop enough strength in the dough during the stretch and folds.

- If the crust is blond (did not caramelize) the oven temperature probably wasn't hot enough, the dough was either over or under fermented, or the bake time wasn't long enough.

- If the crust is burnt, the oven temperature was too hot or you baked it too long.

- If the cheese is broken, the bake time may have been too long (the oven temperature was too low or you left the pizza in too long), you cut the cheese too small, or the cheese quality was poor. Cut the cheese into larger pieces and preheat your oven for longer next time.

- If the sauce is over-reduced, your bake time may have been too long or the sauce was too concentrated when it went on the pizza. Add a bit of water to your tomato sauce before baking the next pie.

PAN PIES

While the round pizza is baked directly on a stone, steel, or hearth, pan pies are, obviously, baked in pans. You must also set the pan on a stone or steel. I love this style of pizza for the shareable, communal experience that it offers. The crust tends to be crispier because it is cooked in an oil slicked pan. My ideal pan pie (one that hits the rubric goals) is a hybrid between the American-Sicilian-style pizza that I grew up on and the Roman pizza in teglia, the latter being lighter, airier, and more aromatic.

You can make a pan pie using any of the dough recipes in Part 3 marked with the pan pie symbol at left. If you would like to make more pan pies than the recipe yields or a different mix of round and pan, simply use Baker's Percentages (see page 142) to scale up the recipe according to your needs.

Pan pies take longer to bake than the round ones because the crust is thicker and the oven temperature is lower (475°F as opposed to 500°F). Plus it takes time to heat up the pan, which, in turn, transfers heat to the dough. Add most toppings midway through the baking process so they don't overcook. During the first phase of baking, the dough is beginning to par-cook. It finishes baking after toppings are added at the 10-minute mark.

I bake pan pies in a 16-inch square pan, but you can use any pan you have, provided it is roughly the same surface area. I use black pans because they absorb and transfer heat more efficiently than shiny metal. The brand I recommend and use is LloydPans, made in Washington State. You can also visit your local restaurant supply store for other options.

To make a pan pie, follow the dough recipes in Part 3 up to the end of Bring the Dough to Room Temperature (page 88), then proceed with the methods below.

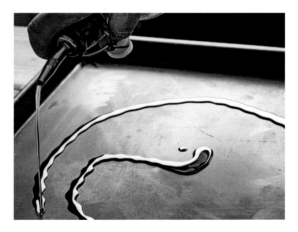

PREHEAT THE OVEN

At least an hour before you plan to bake, preheat your oven to 475°F and place a baking stone or steel 6 to 8 inches below the top of the oven to preheat as well. Oil the pan with extra-virgin olive oil, making sure to hit the sides and corners well before transferring the dough.

STRETCH A PAN
PIZZA

SCAN FOR VIDEO

STRETCH (SHAPE) A PAN PIE

Land the dough onto a very generously floured work surface (or a pan filled with flour for easier cleanup), taking care to track the "top" and "bottom" of your future pizza. You want an ample work surface that will accommodate the dough and toppings. For me, that means at least 3 feet by 3 feet but the bigger the space, the more comfortable you will be stretching the dough. Position the oiled pan on a clean part of your work surface close to where you are shaping the dough. Flour the surface of the dough. Using your fingertips, gently dimple the dough from top to bottom to a uniform thickness. Use the shape of the pan as a visual indicator of the size the dough should be stretched to. Flip the dough over one forearm. Shake it gently to remove excess flour, then gently lower it into the pan. The top of the future pizza is back on top, facing upward.

Use one hand to gently secure the dough in the center of the pan while using your other hand to stretch the dough into the shape of the pan. Using flattened fingertips, fingers together, palms facing upward, pull the dough from the bottom up and over the corners of the pan. Use minimal, quick, decisive movements. The dough may spring back slightly. Repeat with the other side of the dough. Aim for uniform thickness. If the dough is properly relaxed, it should easily stretch to fit the pan's dimensions. If not, cover the pan with a clean kitchen towel and set aside for 10 minutes so the dough can relax.

BUILD

Refer to the toppings in Part 4 (page 169) and multiply the quantity of each by 2.25 to determine how much you need for the pan pie. Prepare them while the oven preheats. Just before baking, add any liquid toppings like tomato sauce, heavy cream, or extra-virgin olive oil to add weight and moisture to the dough so it doesn't puff up in the oven. Save other toppings for later in the bake.

BAKE

Open the oven door and quickly place the pan centered on your stone or steel. Close the door and set a timer for 10 minutes.

Once 10 minutes have passed, quickly remove the pan from the oven and close the door to minimize heat loss. Place the pan on a heatproof work surface. Note if the dough is more caramelized (see page 108) in a certain area and adjust its position, rotating the pan 180 degrees if necessary, when returning to the oven. At this point there shouldn't be any major browning, just a few spots. Add the remaining toppings and return the pan to the stone or steel in the oven to bake until the edges of the pie are browned and the toppings are cooked through, 10 to 12 minutes more.

REST AND EVALUATE

Remove the pan from the oven and place it on a heatproof surface. Using a wide, flat spatula, remove the pizza from the pan and transfer to a wire rack rather than a tabletop to add any additional toppings. This prevents moisture from collecting under the crust, which will dampen and soften it.

Analyze the pan pie based on the Pizza Evaluation Rubric (page xviii).

SLICE, EAT, AND ENJOY

Transfer the pizza to a flat surface and slice it using whatever tool you have handy: scissors, a wheel, or a chef's knife.

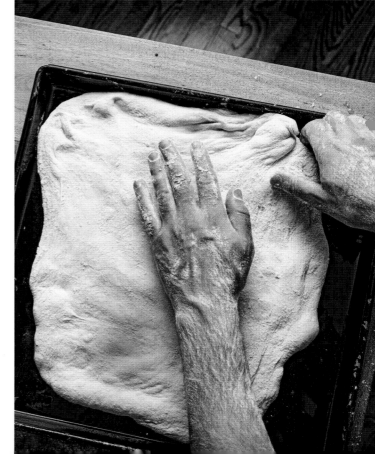

WOOD FIRED MASONRY OVEN BAKING

Masonry ovens are made of stone, brick, concrete, and refractory materials and have an incredible capacity to trap and store heat. Think of them as enclosed fires meant to harness the energy generated by burning wood or gas.

Wood fired ovens offer the possibility of baking pizzas at temperatures that far surpass the typical home oven's 500°F threshold. They rely on three types of heat: conduction (heat directly from the hearth through direct contact with the dough), radiant heat (waves of heat from the fire and the stored heat in the walls), and, to a lesser extent, convection (the air moving in the oven). However, just because they can get up to nearly 1000°F and cook a pizza in under 90 seconds doesn't mean that's the ideal scenario for baking pizzas. In fact, a slightly longer bake at a lower temperature (somewhere in the 600 to 700°F range) can produce a structurally sound, properly cooked pie that will check all the Pizza Evaluation Rubric boxes.

As the wood burns, it draws air in through the oven mouth, feeding the fire. The waves of heat generated by the fire move through the oven interior around and up the dome, eventually exiting from the flue above the mouth. The goal, as the fire burns, is to store as much heat as possible in the refractory material for maximum efficiency while controlling the heat of the fire as it burns.

One of my favorite things about pizza making is the joyful dance between the oven and the dough. Your oven has to be preheated just right and the dough must be in its prime in order to make a truly stellar pie. That's easier to control with a home oven. But wood fired cooking is undeniably fun and exciting. It brings a raw, primitive aspect to pizza making. Knowing your oven and learning to preheat it so it's fired up and ready to go just as the dough enters its prime is a hugely gratifying achievement earned through practice. Harnessing natural elements like fire and wood alongside

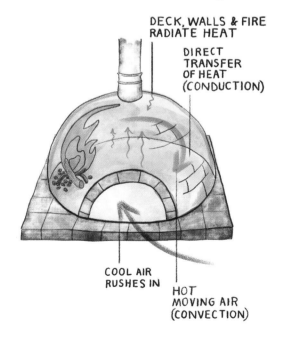

DECK, WALLS & FIRE RADIATE HEAT

DIRECT TRANSFER OF HEAT (CONDUCTION)

COOL AIR RUSHES IN

HOT MOVING AIR (CONVECTION)

the other variables that make pizza excellent is so beautiful to me. I hope you are able to experience it, too.

I recommend wood fired baking for round pies only. Baking pan pizzas in a wood fired or other high temperature oven just doesn't produce the results I am looking for; the temperature is too high and it's too difficult to ensure even baking. Stick to a home oven for those.

KNOW YOUR OVEN: HIGH VS. LOW DOME

When it comes to wood fired baking, the first step is knowing your oven. There are many brands on the market, each offering its own set of off-the-shelf dimensions and many providing custom options.

Neapolitan brands like Acunto and Ferrara have a relatively low dome height, so there is less space for the heat to move, resulting in aggressive heat. Neapolitan ovens rely on fast-moving heat to cook pizzas at very high temperatures, a common feature in restaurant pizza making in the U.S. due to the popularity of the Neapolitan pizza style. It's difficult to create a structurally sound pizza in a Neapolitan oven because the heat is so extreme. The cheese, sauce, and crust cook so quickly that they don't lose their moisture at a rate that a slower bake would. The result is a damp and soupy pizza that must be eaten with a fork and knife.

Italy's Valoriani and Pavesi, France's Le Panyol, and U.S.–made Earth Stone all have higher domes, which translates physically to more space inside the oven, so the heat waves have a greater distance to travel. I prefer a higher dome wood fired oven because it can actually be an incredibly gentle tool for baking pizza once you know how to control the fire.

> Once the logs are lit and combustion is moving along, position the oven door to keep heat in and restrict air flow. Closing the door completely will extinguish the fire. Any time you're not actively baking, keep the door ajar.

PREHEAT THE OVEN AND BUILD YOUR FIRE

I begin by building a fire in the middle of the oven. To start the fire in my 140-centimeter-diameter ovens, I use six logs: two logs (16 inches long and 3 inches maximum in diameter) placed parallel to each other in the middle of the hearth, with two logs stacked perpendicularly on top of those, then another set of two perpendicular logs. To ignite the fire, I use "fatwood," extraordinarily flammable resinous sticks derived from the heartwood of pine trees. Big box stores stock them, but you can use any nontoxic fire starter; never use cardboard because it could be contaminated with glue or other chemicals.

If your oven is smaller than mine, 80 centimeters in diameter, for example, start with just four stacked logs (16 inches long and 3 inches maximum in diameter).

Once the initial fire begins to die down, add logs, one at a time, for 3 to 4 hours to keep the fire going. Your aim is to create a hot, efficient fire that generates enough heat to penetrate deep into the oven's masonry in that time span.

Wood

I honestly and truly feel I can make great pizza with any flour, water, or cheese. But if I have to bake it in a wood fired oven with poor quality wood, I will not be able to deliver. That's one reason gas refractory ovens are as popular as wood fired alternatives. They take out this important variable and impart total control over the heat of the oven, plus they preheat easily. As a die-hard wood fired oven fan, I love the journey of learning an oven and harnessing wood to power it. But I have to admit it is a process to master.

When it comes to baking pizza in a wood fired oven, wood is the single most important ingredient. This might seem self-evident, but for years, I took this for granted because I was always baking with the same wood supply in the same oven at the restaurant. When I started in the business I bought the cheapest wood I could find. I thought it didn't matter. So I purchased wood from a landscaper and seasoned it here in New Jersey. The wood was too moist and was difficult to ignite. I began searching around for alternatives and in the process discovered how important the wood size and moisture are to building a successful fire. It's critical to have a wide range of diameters for the wood for building and maintaining your fire. Use the lowest moisture wood possible so you can create the most efficient fire possible.

Hard Wood vs. Soft Wood

Hard woods come from deciduous trees (trees that lose their leaves and go dormant in the winter). Soft woods, on the other hand, come from evergreens, which are resinous conifers.

Use any hard wood species that you can source reliably. Other than using fatwood to start the fire, do not burn resinous woods such as pine and spruce, because they may have byproducts that produce harmful fumes. They also create more smoke, produce fewer coals, and burn too fast. Hard woods burn cleaner and typically slower. I use birch, maple, beech, and oak, but use whatever is local and available to you.

BTU Maximization

Wood is a natural resource so it makes sense to use it efficiently. Getting the most BTUs (units of heat) for your buck starts with the wood being dry, clean, and positioned properly in the oven. Use an andiron to elevate the wood off the oven deck following the initial preheat so the fire burns efficiently.

Density

This may be hard to believe, but pound for pound, all species of wood will give approximately the same BTUs. Some species are less compact (therefore lighter) so a log of a dense wood would deliver more heat than a less dense log of the same size. Dense wood is also a better value because wood is sold in volumetric measurements like cords, pallets, or cubic feet rather than by weight. And, of course, get whatever fits those parameters and is local—often you won't have a choice of provenance!

Use larger pieces of wood to preheat your oven or to keep the oven hot between long lags in baking. Use the same length but smaller diameter pieces to maintain it. During the bake, use small logs for maximum control over your fire. If your logs are too large, they will emit a lot of BTUs as they burn, generating extreme radiant heat. This will throw your conductive and radiant heat out of balance and the end result could be under- or overcooked pizza. Smaller pieces give you more control over the burn, but they also require more labor to produce so they are slightly more expensive. You can split large pieces down to size with a splitting axe. It's so gratifying to split your own logs! I'm obsessed with my Fiskars x 25.

Moisture

Wood, by nature, is moist. For most of its life, it was absorbing water from the ground through its roots. Losing that moisture takes time (or a kiln). Moisture is the biggest consideration in maximizing your BTUs. If wood is humid, it steals energy to burn moisture off that would otherwise be producing heat.

I recommend kiln-dried wood, which has been dried out in an oven at a low temperature to eliminate moisture and kill pests. Store it indoors or well-covered outdoors to prevent it from getting rained on. It's readily available at big box stores. To get a sense of what dried wood feels like, bang together two logs and commit the hollow thud to memory. Use that memory to assess logs when you don't have a moisture meter or other reliable source for judging moisture.

Avoid using green wood (freshly cut logs), which contains a lot of moisture. Before you purchase seasoned wood (that which has been cut and left to dry naturally for an undetermined amount of time), speak with the vendor and ensure that it is completely dry and has a low moisture content. I highly recommend cultivating a relationship with your local wood purveyor if you can.

Moist wood doesn't ignite as easily or burn as well. If you're unsure of a wood's moisture content, you can buy a hard wood moisture meter online for about $15. Insert the prongs into various logs. I aim for 15 percent at the most. If you don't have a meter, visible splitting at the ends of the log is a good indication of dryness.

Man-Made Alternatives

In addition to natural wood, I sometimes use a compressed product made from wood fibers. My go-to brand is Il Faggetto, imported from Italy. It's reliable, predictable, food safe, totally natural, and has less than 8 percent moisture. As a bonus it comes in a cardboard box so it's easy to stack and move, a major plus for a restaurant with limited storage. Most wood fired pizzerias in the United States source wood locally (olive wood in California, for example), but I have seen a lot of man-made wood products in Europe, where they are more attentive to ecologically sound alternatives to hard wood. I hope the U.S. gets on board someday, too.

Storage

When you purchase your wood, arrange your stack by size, separating the large and small pieces. Keep the wood as dry as possible. If you store it outdoors, cover it loosely with a tarp or keep it in a shed sheltered from the elements but open to air flow.

Preheating Times

So much of pizza making is about maximizing thermal mass—storing heat in your oven's hearth—and transferring that heat into the pizza over time. Wood fired ovens aren't like a stove you can turn on and off or adjust quickly and use to cook predictably. Instead, you have to build sustained heat in order to penetrate the depths of the floor and the walls.

One great benefit of having a restaurant where we build a fire every day is that the oven never fully cools down, so we aren't starting from ambient temperature each time we preheat the oven. The oven may still retain 500°F from the previous night's service, which drastically reduces the length of time needed to preheat the oven—to around just 45 minutes.

Heating a cold oven takes much longer. Depending on your oven and its thermal mass, you may need to preheat your oven for 4 hours, or even longer. Your oven builder should be able to provide you with specifications for your model. Regardless, there's no shortcut for building sustained heat deep in the hearth, so budget plenty of time before you plan to bake.

DETERMINE WHEN YOUR OVEN IS READY

It would be a bit misleading to give you a target temperature for your wood fired oven. First of all, the nature of the oven means that there will be a range of temperatures present across the hearth, varying sometimes as much as 200°F between the temperature at the mouth and the temperature closest to the fire. Rather than give you a strict number to aim for, I recommend using visual indicators, with caveats, to determine when your oven is ready.

The best indicator in my opinion is the color of the inside of the dome. When you first start your fire, the dome will turn from gray to black as the wood releases creosote, which sticks to the oven's dome. As the oven temp increases, that layer burns off and the refractory material appears gray again. That's a good indication that the surface of your oven is hot, but the only way to know if the hearth is deeply preheated is to give it a long preheat and to bake on it.

Another option (though I don't recommend it) for gauging your oven temperature is to use a temperature "gun." This infrared thermometer uses a laser to focus the thermometer's lens, which in turn infers and interprets the thermal radiation coming off a surface, displaying the corresponding temperature. I'm not a big fan of infrared thermometers because they tell you the surface temperature of an oven deck, but with no indication of how deep the heat has penetrated into the oven's masonry.

Rather than relying on tools, I think it's important to get to know your oven, be intuitive, and embrace the tradition of wood fired cooking that predates modern technology. It takes time and practice, but as you get to know your oven you begin to think of it not just in the moment, but what temperatures there will be in which locations on the deck over the hours your fire is preheating, burning, and dying and how much stored heat you have to work with, a sort of temperature timeline. It's a beautiful process.

TRANSFER THE FIRE

Once the oven is preheated on the surface and deep in the masonry, use a metal turning peel and oven rake to move the fire to 3 or 9 o'clock. Choose a side based on where it's most comfortable to stand as you load the oven. If your pizza station or landscaping is on the right and you can't comfortably stand there, you must load from the left; the fire must be on the right. Elevate the wood with an andiron so air flows around it evenly and it combusts as efficiently as possible. You're paying for your fuel source so you want it to burn, not smolder, for maximum effect.

Burn, Baby, Burn

I often find that when ovens are too hot or too cold, it's because the person tending the fire hasn't taken the time to really get to know the oven or that batch of wood. If it's your first time or you have limited experience with wood fired cooking, do yourself a favor: Spend a few days building fires in the oven and just feeding them and watching them burn. You may terrify your neighbors but you'll learn a lot through observation. We recently installed a second oven at Razza, a souped up version of the first. Still, I treated it as a whole different beast and spent every day for weeks building fires and cooking pizzas in order to acquaint myself with it. Only through repetition and attention was I able to dial in the oven and understand how it heats, how it cools, and the size of the fire it requires.

Next, build some fires and blind bake (bake without any toppings) some pizza dough just to see how it behaves while baking. Shape the dough and land it in different parts of the oven to see how it springs (or doesn't), caramelizes (or doesn't), and generally behaves on different parts of the deck.

What to Do If Your Oven Is Too Hot

Let's say you have a wood fired oven that's just way too hot, like when you heat a cast iron skillet to make pancakes and it's beyond smoking by the time you're ready to cook. In the case of the cast iron, you have the option to turn down the heat and wait it out. A wood fired oven has several inches of heated material, plus a thermal blanket of insulation, so it's going to take quite a bit longer for it to cool down. The quickest way to cool off the oven deck is to bake on it.

A pizza draws heat off the deck as it cooks. If you have pizza dough to burn, you can cool the oven by cooking and burning pies (this is more feasible for a pizzeria that has lots of dough on hand and needs its oven to reach the right temperature for service). Otherwise, throw a tray of vegetables or meatballs into the oven to roast, don't feed the fire, and wait for the oven to cool off. Removing logs and embers does nothing to cool off the stored heat of the oven, which is the source you are looking to diminish.

What to Do If Your Oven Is Too Cold

If your oven is too cold, it's more difficult to pivot than if it's too hot. You just have to build a bigger fire and it could take hours from when you start, so put the dough in the refrigerator to prevent it from overproofing. It's key to manage your oven temperature in a way that it's preheated at the same time the dough is proofed and ready to bake.

MAINTAIN THE FIRE

Once your fire is at 3 or 9 o'clock, keeping it going while the pizza bakes is a matter of adding logs of similar length (16 inches) but smaller diameter (1½ inches for a smaller oven, 2 to 2.5 inches for a larger oven) than you used for the preheat, one piece at a time. Monitor the flames. A robust fire will have flames curling up just to the center of the dome. Only bake pizza when you have that scenario. When the flames subside, add another log, then bake when the flames curl up toward the center of the dome again.

LOAD THE OVEN

Build your pizza on the floured peel (see page 104). Be sure to jiggle the peel a bit before launching the pizza to be sure it isn't sticking to the peel. Launch the dough into place by quickly pulling the peel away as you load the dough onto the deck. If your fire is at 3 o'clock, drop your dough at 10 or 11 o'clock a few inches from the wall. If your fire is burning at 9 o'clock, drop your dough at 1 or 2 o'clock a few inches from the wall. With time, you will learn the precise distance from the wall and fire that cooks the pizza most evenly, and with experience you will be able to accurately land the pizza exactly where you intended.

Unlike a home oven, which may not give you a clear view of the pizza as it bakes, a wood fired oven's open mouth lets you observe the pizza every step of the way. The wall is radiating heat, so if the pizza is too close it will burn.

LOAD THE OVEN

SCAN FOR VIDEO

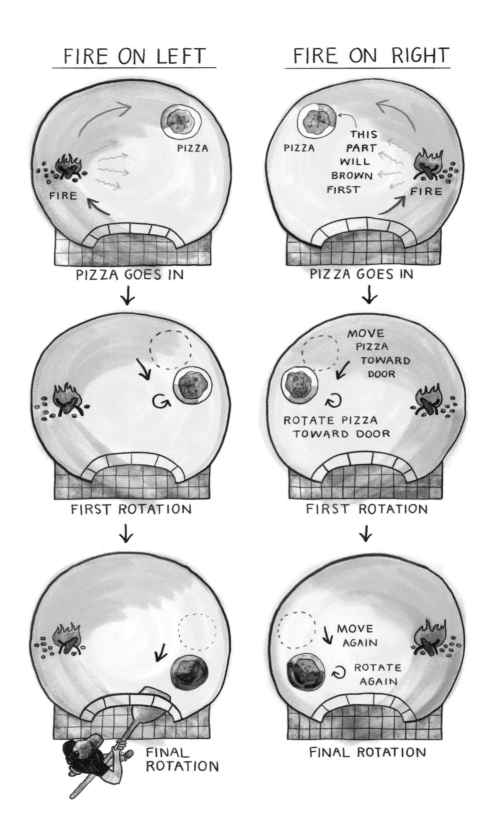

BAKE

Upon landing on the deck, the entire rim of the pizza should begin to swell as oven spring (see page 108) occurs. A properly executed dough will show signs of oven spring within 30 seconds of landing on the oven deck. If not, your oven may be too cold or your dough could be over or under fermented.

For wood fired cooking, the floor is a major contributor to oven spring, and it works in tandem with the radiant heat waves and convection. I land my pizza on the opposite side of the oven from the fire. The heat waves moving around the oven and direct contact with the hot oven floor conspire with the fire's flames to give this giant burst of heat needed to spring the pizza.

Next, look for signs of caramelization (light browning and wisps of smoke and steam are early indications). Based on the physics of the oven, as well as the dough's proximity to the fire, the first third of the rim will caramelize first (from about 7 to 11 o'clock if the fire is on the left side of the oven, 1 to 5 o'clock if it is on the right). If the sides are getting charred or burned instead of caramelizing, just throw out the pizza. If you proceed with the next two movements the pizza will be completely burnt by the time you do a full revolution.

Once the first third just begins to show signs of caramelization, use a peel to turn the pizza in the direction of the fire (counterclockwise if the fire is on the left, clockwise if it is on the right), moving it slightly closer to the door (see illustration on opposite page). Once the second third is caramelized, turn the dough once again, moving it closer still to the door, and bake until the rim is fully caramelized. As the pizza bakes, use the peel frequently to lift it up to observe signs of caramelization on the undercarriage as well.

Understanding the thermodynamics of convection is really helpful. You have this invisible hot air moving, following the shape of the oven (clockwise if the fire's on the left; counterclockwise if the fire is on the right). With experience, you will intuitively know the whole spectrum of temperatures of your oven and how to use them, from the hottest (next to the fire) to coolest (at the oven door).

JUDGE WHEN THE PIZZA IS DONE

For determining when a pizza is ready, observe the level of caramelization of the crust and the undercarriage, as well as cheese melting and sauce reduction. If the crust and undercarriage are baking too quickly and burning, you may have to cool down your oven. If the cheese is breaking (see page 35), cut it into larger pieces for your next pizza. If the sauce is over-reduced, thin it with a bit of water before the next bake. Make these same observations with each bake and make any adjustments accordingly.

Use the peel to remove the pizza from the oven and then follow the instructions for resting and slicing (page 112).

POST BAKE

- Use residual heat to cook other things
- Let the fire burn out
- Clean the oven

Using the Peel to Your Advantage

Check the pizza's undercarriage as it bakes: Slide the peel beneath the pizza, dip your body as you tip the pizza slightly, and observe the appearance of the undercarriage.

If the bottom of your pizza is getting burned, dome it: Use the peel to raise the pizza to just below the apex of the dome to finish any melting and complete the caramelization with it elevated.

If you observe debris like ash, burnt flour, or burnt cheese on the bottom of the pizza, brush it off and use a brass bristle brush to clean the oven deck. To prevent debris from building up, you should brush your baking steel, pizza stone, or oven deck after every few pizzas.

Undercarriage, from blond to burnt

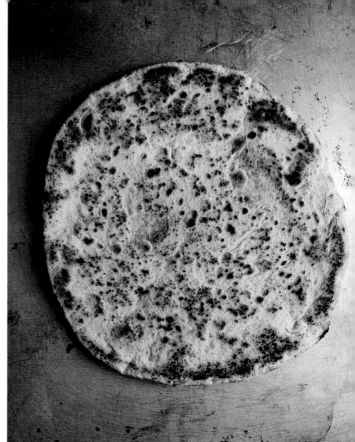

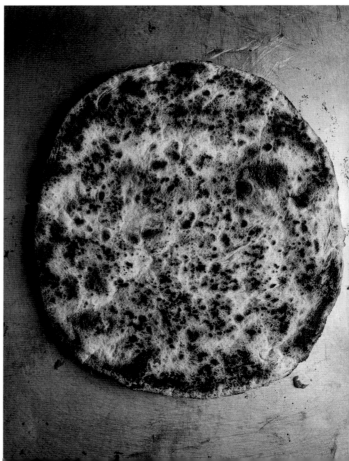

Ideal

This is burnt. Do not eat!

This is extremely burnt. Do not eat!

Baking with an Ooni, Roccbox, Breville Pizzaiolo, or Other Small High Temperature Oven

Building a wood fired oven in your backyard could easily set you back $12,000 to $15,000. For your sake, I hope you can afford it. But for the rest of us in search of heat a bit higher than what a home oven can offer, there are a number of high heat ovens on the market that are significantly more affordable, along with being more portable.

You can bake any of the doughs made for high temperature ovens marked with the symbol at right in the Ooni, Roccbox, and Breville Pizzaiolo portable pizza ovens. Bear in mind that, like a wood burning oven, you don't need to use the highest possible heat to get excellent results. In fact, because these ovens are so small, the heat is more intense, so you have more control over the bake if you run the ovens at 600 to 700°F instead of the hottest setting. The key to success with any of them is to really get to know your oven through practice. It will take many bakes to dial in your settings. Always note your temperature settings and stick with them!

Ooni makes gas, wood, and charcoal-fueled ovens ($249 to $599) that direct flames toward the top of a domed steel oven, providing a searing top heat and good bottom heat. Temperatures reach up to 930°F but pizzas cook more evenly below 700°F (I play with the dial and guesstimate for this temperature). Due to the heat element's position and a wide open mouth, you have to negotiate temperature gradients within the oven. One way to mitigate this temperature inconsistency is to do a preheat of at least 30 minutes. I like the larger size of the Ooni Pro model, which provides a slightly more gentle heat and accommodates 12-inch pies. For outdoor use only.

Gozney's Roccbox ($499) is a tabletop, gas-powered oven that can produce similar results as the Ooni. It's supremely light and portable so it's great for pop-ups. The heat element is at the back and directs the heat to the top of the dome, providing a consistent top heat. The part of the oven closest to the flame is so close to the edge of your pizza that you will have to consistently turn the pizza to get an evenly cooked rim and to avoid burning it. The Gozney Dome ($1,499) is a low domed 16-inch wood or gas powered oven that mimics the design of a Neapolitan oven. For outdoor use only.

Breville's Pizzaiolo ($999) is an electric oven designed for indoor use. It has heat elements on the top and bottom heating up to 750°F and features a Hack Mode, allowing autonomous temperature settings for both elements and guaranteeing maximum control over your bake. For the best results with the doughs in this book, run the top and bottom elements at 600 to 700°F.

PART 3

PIZZA DOUGH RECIPES

The dough recipes in this chapter are listed in order of ascending difficulty, beginning with My Everyday Dough. It takes three days from start to finish, but it is made with white flour and commercial yeast so it has a much lower learning curve than the recipes that follow it, which feature whole wheat and high extraction flour, sourdough starter, or freshly milled grains.

I recommend starting with My Everyday Dough, even if you're an experienced baker. It will give you the opportunity to practice with a relatively high hydration dough (it weighs in at 76 percent), which is a little bit more challenging to work with and takes some time to get used to—but it's worth it! Whether you make My Everyday Dough or advanced level "Choose Your Own Adventure" Dough, you can make pizza that lives up to the standards of the Pizza Evaluation Rubric (page xviii), albeit with different flavors if you are using yeast versus natural leavening.

Each recipe includes a number of figures before the procedures. The first is the yield, the number of round or square pies the ingredient quantities that follow will produce. Next is the desired dough temperature. Use this figure in the formula in each recipe to determine the temperature of the water to use when mixing dough.

The figures that follow are Baker's Percentages (see page 142), proportions that are essential to professional bakers and can be adopted at home as well. An experienced baker can look at those percentages and immediately know the dough's hydration and salt content in order to evaluate whether they want to continue with the recipe. Any serious baker will want to know all those specs before undertaking a three-day dough commitment. Baker's Percentages are indispensable for scaling up a recipe, particularly when you intend to mix dough for a combination of round and pan pies, which have different dough ball weights. Then, when you begin to develop your own recipes, you can use the Baker's Percentages as a template, tweaking ingredient proportions to experiment for different outcomes.

For the yeasted and sourdough recipes, I also include the Total Formula, which tallies the total amount of each ingredient, like total flour weight (the dry flour and the pre-fermented flour in the starter, if using), and total water weight (the amount of water in the Final Mix and in the starter, if using), yeast, and salt.

For sourdough recipes, I include the Final Mix, which is a list of ingredients that you will combine to execute the recipe. It is the litany of items that you will actually mix together, whereas the Total Formula is more like your shopping list.

For recipes that use starter, I include instructions for the final feeding to be done the day you intend to mix the dough. Be sure your starter is already very active before attempting to mix dough with it.

Each recipe is accompanied by symbols indicating whether it is suited for round pizzas , pan pies , home ovens , or high-temperature ovens .

Use gram measurements for all dough recipes. You will need two metric scales, one for measuring yeast to fractions of a gram, the other for measuring flour, water, salt, and starter (if using) in grams.

Each recipe is divided into days and stages. The stages like Incorporate Ingredients and Autolyse (or Resting Period) are related to the dough mixing, shaping, and baking concepts laid out in Part 2. Before attempting to mix the dough, read Part 2 thoroughly and view the accompanying technique videos accessed by scanning the QR codes.

Transfer Loss

When mixing dough, a small amount will stick to your hands and the bowl, resulting in a final dough weight that is slightly less than the sum of the ingredients' weights. The bowl residue, so-called transfer loss, will depend on the size of your bowl, the size of your batch, and how much dough remains stuck to your hands. For small batches in a home setting, 2 to 3 percent loss is pretty average. So don't be alarmed if the last dough ball you weigh comes up a little short in the weight department. This is normal. If you want, you can multiply the ingredients in your final mix by 1.02 or 1.03 percent to offset the inevitable transfer loss.

Baker's Percentages

Baker's Percentages are the single most useful tool at my disposal when initially approaching a recipe and I list them at the beginning of each dough recipe. These numbers tell the proportional relationship between flour, water, salt, and yeast. Whether you're making two dough balls or 2,000, the Baker's Percentages stay the same. Unlike the recipes, which are rooted in fixed quantities, they are rooted in relationships. This isn't like algebra class, where you wonder when on earth you're ever going to use this math. With time and practice, mastering baker's math becomes second nature and makes you a better baker so you will be able to bring even more joy to your table in the form of great pizza!

Baker's Percentages are useful for beginner bakers, too, because once you understand them, you will have a deeper comprehension of dough, its components, and how they work together. The most critical numbers for developing, managing, and improving upon my dough recipe lie in this baker's math. For any student of fractions (or eaters of pies!), the numbers listed in the Baker's Percentage section may seem strange at first. First of all, the percentages don't add up to 100! (I explain that below.) But here's what you'll do with these numbers: First determine the amount (weight) of dough you want. Then figure out the unit value of a percentage point and multiply each percentage by the unit value to get the weight to use for each ingredient.

Take My Everyday Dough recipe (page 146), for example:

    100% white flour
    76% water
    2% salt
    0.3% instant yeast
    =178.3%

UNDERSTANDING A YEASTED RECIPE:

Flour is always 100%. The other ingredients are expressed in proportion to the flour.

FLOUR
100%

WATER
76%

SALT
2%

YEAST
0.3%

Baker's math always adds up to more than 100%. It's not your typical idea of a "percent."

adds up to

178.3

TOTAL BAKER'S UNITS FOR THIS RECIPE

The total percentage of all ingredients is 178.3 percent. Baker's Percentages are always based on the ratio of flour (100 percent) to the other ingredients, so the total percentages will inevitably add up to far more than 100 percent. While this does not seem straightforward at first, once you get the hang of it, this method of expressing ingredients allows you to customize the recipe to adapt to your own conditions, schedule, and desire to create something new and unique.

For recipes that incorporate starter, you use a similar approach but you must account for the pre-fermented flour and water in the starter. This is the only way to ensure the hydration of your dough is accurate. All of the starters in this book are 100 percent hydration, containing equal parts flour and water. That means 250 grams of starter, for example, contains 125 grams each of flour and water.

Let's say you're hosting a party and you want to make 15 sourdough pizzas from balls weighing 250 grams each. If you're using the Baker's Percentages from the illustration below, here's how you do the math for that particular scenario:

> 100% flour (90% white flour,
>   10% whole wheat flour)
> 76% water
> 2% salt
> =178%

Multiply 15 by 250 to determine the total dough weight. The result is 3750 grams. Then divide that number by the total baker's units (178) to ascertain the unit value [3750 ÷ 178] = 21.07. In other words, each of the 178 percentage points is "worth" 21.07 Applying the math we used above, the Total Formula is:

(Continued)

UNDERSTANDING A STARTER-BASED RECIPE:

Here's the total formula (all the flour and water, including that which is in the starter, and salt).

FLOUR
100%

WATER
76%

SALT
2%

Let's say a recipe calls for 10% pre-fermented flour. To account for the flour and water in the starter, subtract 10% flour and 10% water from the total formula's flour weight and water weight.

−10%

FLOUR
100%

−10%

WATER
76%

+20%

STARTER
20%

SALT
2%

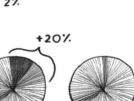

Remember that my starter is equal parts flour and water.

2107 grams flour [100 x 21.07]
1601 grams water [76 x 21.07]
42 grams salt [2 x 21.07]

Since we know the recipe is 10 percent pre-fermented flour in the form of starter, we can multiply the total flour weight by 0.1 and find the amount of flour in the starter [2107 x 0.1] = 211 grams. Since the starter for the recipe is 100 percent hydration, we know the water in the starter also weighs 211 grams. Therefore, we must subtract 211 grams each from the total flour weight and the total water weight to determine the remaining flour and water in the recipe:

1896 grams white flour
1390 grams water
422 grams starter
42 grams salt

This is the Final Mix for making 15 round pies, each weighing 250 grams. You can apply this math for scaling up recipes or ascertaining ingredient quantities for a mix of round and pan pies.

Using Baker's Percentages you can accurately scale up any recipe to create as many dough balls as you need. To do so, start with two fixed variables: how many dough balls (and therefore pizzas) you want to make and how much they should weigh. Let's say I want to make three 900-gram pan pies following My Everyday Dough recipe. Using these numbers and the recipe's Baker's Percentages, I can apply simple calculations to ascertain exactly how much each of flour, water, yeast, and salt I am going to need to execute the recipe.

Multiply 3 by 900 to determine the total dough weight. The result is 2700 grams. Then divide that number by the total baker's units (178.3) to ascertain the unit value: [2700 ÷ 178.3] = 15.14. In other words, each of the 178.3 percentage points is "worth" 15.14.

Next, multiply the unit value by each percentage: 100 for flour, 76 for water, 2 for salt, and 0.3 for yeast. The results are the quantities of each ingredient you need to make three (900-gram) pan pie dough balls:

1514 grams flour [100 x 15.14]
1150 grams water [76 x 15.14]
30.3 grams salt [2 x 15.14]
4.5 grams instant yeast [0.3 x 15.14]

Once you have mastered this math, you can make any dough recipe at any scale you wish. This is particularly useful if you want to make dough for multiple round and pan pies, which weigh 200 to 275 grams (depending on the oven) and 850 to 900 grams, respectively. Then if you wish to customize the formula (change the hydration or salt, for example) you can adjust those percentages slightly to get the results you want (a less hydrated dough for high temperature ovens or a more seasoned dough with a slightly higher salt content, for example).

SCALING A RECIPE TO MAKE ANY NUMBER OF PIZZAS OF ANY SIZE:

 Decide how many pizzas you want, and how big you want each pizza to be. This is particularly useful if you want to make a bigger or smaller pizza. You can increase or decrease the dough ball weight according to your needs. The number of pizzas times the pizza dough ball weight equals the total dough weight.

HOW MANY PIZZAS YOU WANT **X** GRAMS OF DOUGH PER PIZZA **=** TOTAL DOUGH WEIGHT

 Divide your answer by the total baker's units for the recipe. The answer is the unit value for your new, customized recipe.

TOTAL DOUGH WEIGHT **÷** TOTAL BAKER'S UNITS **=** UNIT VALUE

 Multiply the unit value by each baker's percentage of the original recipe. The recipe is now scaled to your needs!

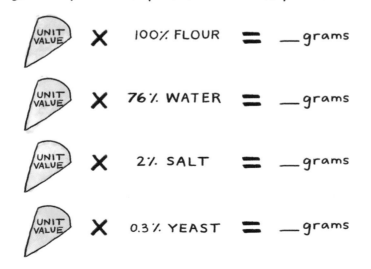

UNIT VALUE **X** 100% FLOUR **=** __grams

UNIT VALUE **X** 76% WATER **=** __grams

UNIT VALUE **X** 2% SALT **=** __grams

UNIT VALUE **X** 0.3% YEAST **=** __grams

MY EVERYDAY DOUGH

NAME YOUR INTENTION:
Make a pizza using basic ingredients available at any supermarket, build confidence with managing fermentation, train your hands to handle high hydration doughs, understand the idiosyncrasies of your home oven, practice launching high hydration doughs.

This is the simplest of the dough recipes and also the most flexible. This is not the Razza dough; this is my everyday dough, the one that I always have in my refrigerator at home, just waiting. It's part of my family's daily life and, to be honest, it's so versatile that I can't even confine it to pizza. I use it for ciabatta, English muffins, even a boule. It is made with white flour and commercial yeast (I like Saf brand), so it's straightforward and approachable. You can use any run-of-the-mill flour from the supermarket and still get great flavor and results that will hit many of the notes and characteristics I lay out in the Pizza Evaluation Rubric (the starter-based recipes that follow will yield more complex flavors, however). This dough recipe is designed for the home oven. Modify the recipe according to the instructions on page 149 to bake in a high temperature oven.

Don't stress about the fact that the method that follows takes three days from start to finish. I highly recommend taking this time to develop flavor in the dough. Once the initial mixing is done, the successive steps take 5 minutes or less each until you're ready to bake. Most of the time, the dough is fermenting on your counter or in the refrigerator.

Besides its versatility, what I love most about this recipe is that it provides training for beginner and intermediate level bakers' hands and will help build confidence with handling delicate, high hydration dough (this one is 76 percent), which requires a bit of practice to do without tearing, overhandling, or degassing. Once you're ready to move on to a slightly more complex dough, try the Yeasted Whole Wheat, High Extraction, or Freshly Milled Flour Dough (page 150), which uses commercial yeast and 20 percent whole wheat flour, which is a little more difficult to work with.

Makes 7 balls weighing about 250 grams each for round pizza; or 2 balls weighing about 890 grams each for pan pizza.

Desired dough temperature: 78°F

INGREDIENTS	BAKER'S PERCENTAGES	TOTAL FORMULA
White flour (all-purpose or bread flour), plus more for dusting	100%	1000 grams
Water	76%	760 grams
Fine sea salt	2%	20 grams
Instant yeast	0.3%	3 grams
Extra-virgin olive oil, for oiling		
Rice flour, for dusting the peel		
TOTAL	178.3%	1783 grams

DAY 1

Calculate Target Water Temperature: Measure the room temperature and the temperature of the flour and use the formula to determine the water temperature:

(78°F x 3) − (Air Temperature + Flour Temperature + Friction Factor*) = Target Water Temperature (°F)

*If you're mixing by hand, the Friction Factor will be close to 0. If you're using a mixer, use the instructions on page 73 to determine the Friction Factor.

Weigh Your Ingredients.

Incorporate Ingredients: In a large bowl, mix together the flour and yeast. Add the water and mix with your fingertips or a spoon until no dry bits remain.

Resting Period: Set aside, covered with a clean kitchen towel, for 20 minutes to 1 hour to hydrate the flour.

Incorporate the Salt: Uncover the bowl. Sprinkle over the salt and use your fingers to scissor pinch it into the dough. I use my thumb and first finger to work the salt in from one side of the dough to the next.

Knead: Once the salt is incorporated and dissolved, use four closed fingers, pinky to index, and mix using the Rubaud method: Secure the bowl with your nondominant hand. Scoop your hand under the far end of the dough, lift slightly, drop, and scoop again. Repeat the scooping/digging motion, turning the bowl slightly every four or five scoops. Mix until the dough comes together, becomes uniform, and tightens up, 5 to 7 minutes.

Bulk Ferment with Stretch and Folds: Transfer the dough to a clean, very lightly oiled plastic or glass bowl. Set aside, covered with plastic wrap or a clean kitchen towel, at room temperature for 30 minutes.

After 30 minutes, uncover the bowl. Place a small bowl of cold water next to the dough bowl. Stretch and fold the dough in the bowl to develop more strength. Every time you touch the dough, dip your hand in the water first. Starting at 12 o'clock, pull the quadrant of dough upward gently 6 to 12 inches (as much as the dough allows without tearing), then press it gently onto itself. Turn the bowl a half turn and repeat. Next, turn the bowl a quarter turn and repeat the lifting/pressing, then a half turn and repeat. The dough will tighten up and get stronger during the series of stretch and folds. Set aside, covered with plastic wrap or a clean kitchen towel, at room temperature, for another 30 minutes.

Repeat the stretch and folds every 30 minutes. After 2 hours from the beginning of bulk fermentation, the dough should feel like there's a bit of gas building up in it, and it should pass the Window Pane Test (see page 75). Cover with plastic wrap and place in the refrigerator to rest overnight. If it feels like there's no gas production after 2 hours, set the bowl aside until the dough has increased in volume by at least 20 percent before transferring to the refrigerator. Overnight there will be a little more gas development.

Using a Mixer: Yeasted Dough

When using a mixer for this or other high hydration yeasted dough recipes (anything above 70 percent), use the double hydration technique (see page 66), adding 85 percent of the water by weight to the mixing bowl first, followed by the flour and yeast mixture. Mix until shaggy, rest, covered, for 20 minutes to 1 hour, then incorporate the salt and continue mixing until the dough exhibits medium gluten development (see page 74). Then add the remaining water slowly. As soon as the water is fully incorporated, turn off the mixer. Transfer the dough to a very lightly oiled container and follow the recipe procedure above beginning from the Bulk Ferment with Stretch and Folds step.

Using a mixer can reduce the number of total stretch and folds in order to reach the desired stage of gluten development, so you may only need to do one series. Bulk fermentation is complete when the dough has increased in volume by at least 20 percent and passes the Window Pane Test.

DAY 2

The Next Morning (or at least 12 hours later), remove the bowl from the refrigerator and uncover. Stretch and fold the dough once more in the bowl. The dough will feel stronger. Cover with plastic wrap and return to the refrigerator.

Divide and Round: Before bed (or at least 12 hours later), remove the bowl from the refrigerator and uncover. Turn the dough out onto a lightly floured work surface, allowing it to gently release from the bowl. Handle the dough with extreme care. Using a dough scraper, cut the dough into seven equal pieces weighing about 250 grams each. If you are making a pan pie, cut the dough into two equal pieces weighing about 890 grams each.

Working with one piece of dough, bring the top half of the dough (from 12 o'clock) and lift and press it into the center of the dough. Next, bring the bottom half of the dough and lift and press it into the center. Take the left side of the dough and lift and press it into the center. Repeat with the right side. Then, take four corners and pull and fold them into the center of the ball and gently press to attach. Do not flatten. Be sure the ball is round and the bottom is sealed, pinching it closed if necessary. Gently flip the dough seam-side down. Repeat this process with the remaining dough pieces.

Place each ball into individual, very lightly oiled plastic containers large enough to allow the ball to double in volume. You can also place the balls in a lightly floured dough tray or baking sheet, dust their surface with flour, and cover with plastic wrap.

Proof: Transfer the dough to the refrigerator to rest overnight (or for at least 12 hours).

DAY 3

Bring the Dough to Room Temperature: The next day (or at least 12 hours later), 2 to 3 hours before stretching and baking, remove the dough from the refrigerator and set it aside to reach room temperature. The dough should have substantially increased in volume in the refrigerator. If it has not, allow it to increase in volume at room temperature before baking. The dough is ready when it has increased in volume by 20 percent and passes the Poke Test (springs back slowly and leaves a slight indentation when poked, page 89).

Preheat Your Oven: At least 1 hour before baking, preheat the oven to 500°F and set a baking stone or steel on a rack 6 to 8 inches below the top of the oven to preheat as well. You want the oven as hot as possible, so turn the broiler on during the last 10 minutes if your oven allows. Turn off the broiler before you load the oven.

Stretch: Flour the top of a dough ball. If it is in a container, turn the dough out onto a generously floured surface. If it is in a dough tray or resting on a baking sheet, with your nondominant hand resting gently on top of the floured dough ball, use a dough scraper to scoop up the dough. Then invert the dough and gently land it on a generously floured surface. Try not to damage any of the structure at all, and be as minimally invasive as possible. Keep track of the "top" and "bottom" of the dough. The top of your future pizza is the one currently facing the countertop.

Using extremely gentle movements with flat fingertips spread, apply pressure on the dough at 10 and 2 o'clock. Lift your hands and reposition on the dough closer to you. Move from the top of the dough toward you, pressing downward and outward. Leave an inch along the rim that you don't touch at all.

Flip the dough over. The top of the future pizza is now facing upward. Continue stretching the dough, using the technique that works best for you. One approach is to leave the dough on the counter and, with one hand in the center, pull at 3, 6, 9, and 12 o'clock. Another is to scoop up the dough from below with your palms facing the counter, then turn the dough, stretching and pulling it in increments with your knuckles. Be super gentle and don't be afraid to rely on gravity, a great stretcher of pizza dough. Regardless of your technique, stretch the dough until you get to a 10- to 11-inch diameter. You will stretch it to a 12-inch diameter on the peel.

If making a pan pie, shape and bake the dough according to the instructions on page 118.

Pause and Assess.

Transfer to the Peel: Dust the peel with coarse rice flour. Next, wipe your hands to remove any excess moisture. Gently scoop up the dough, sliding your hands beneath it, palms facing the work surface. Shake off any excess flour and transfer the dough to the floured peel. Using flattened and spread fingertips, palms facing upward from underneath, gently pull the dough until the disk reaches 12 inches in diameter. Be sure your hands are dry when you do this, otherwise the dough will stick to the peel.

Build: Add your desired toppings from a recipe in Part 4 (page 169).

Bake: Bake according to the method on page 111 at 500°F for 6 to 7 minutes.

Rest and Evaluate: Analyze the pizza according to the Pizza Evaluation Rubric (page xviii) and take notes so your next bake is even better.

Slice, Eat, and Enjoy!

Repeat with remaining dough balls, allowing your stone or steel to adequately recover between bakes.

Adapting Dough for High Temperature Ovens

 To modify My Everyday Dough for baking in a high temperature oven, simply reduce the hydration to 68 percent. In other words, use 680 grams of water instead of 760 grams. If using a wood fired oven, aim for dough balls weighing 250 to 270 grams. For smaller models of the tabletop high temperature ovens, which accommodate smaller pies, aim for 200-gram balls.

YEASTED WHOLE WHEAT, HIGH EXTRACTION, OR FRESHLY MILLED FLOUR DOUGH

NAME YOUR INTENTION:
Gain confidence working with whole wheat, high extraction, or freshly milled flour, add additional flavor to your yeasted dough.

Once you have a handle on My Everyday Dough (page 146), a 100 percent white flour recipe, you can apply the techniques you have learned to create this slightly more complex dough made with whole wheat, high extraction, or freshly milled flour. The bran and germ in these types of flours give doughs more flavor, complexity, and nutrition: You will immediately taste and smell the difference in the finished product, which will be more fragrant than My Everyday Dough. The flours also add a level of difficulty because the bran's sharp edges inhibit gluten development, so working with them to create a satisfying dough requires a little more skill, as well as restraint.

I generally use a maximum of 20 percent whole wheat, high extraction, or freshly milled flour in

my doughs. High extraction T85 flour is a favorite of mine. If you're new to the art of whole wheat, high extraction, or freshly milled flour baking, start with a lower proportion of it and work your way up incrementally from there. Begin with just 5 percent by weight. That means 50 grams of whole wheat flour and 950 grams of white flour. Work up to 10 percent (100 grams whole wheat to 900 grams white flour), then 15 percent (150 grams whole wheat to 850 grams white flour).

Makes 7 balls weighing about 255 grams each for round pizza; or 2 balls weighing about 900 grams each for pan pizza.

Desired dough temperature: 78°F

INGREDIENTS	BAKER'S PERCENTAGES	TOTAL FORMULA
White flour (all-purpose or bread flour), plus more for dusting	80%	800 grams
Whole grain, high extraction, or freshly milled flour of your choice	20%	200 grams
Water	78%	780 grams
Fine sea salt	2%	20 grams
Instant yeast	0.3%	3 grams
Extra-virgin olive oil, for oiling		
Rice flour, for dusting the peel		
Total	180.3%	1803 grams

DAY 1

Calculate Target Water Temperature: Measure the room temperature and the temperature of the flour and use the formula below to determine the water temperature.

(78°F x 3) − (Air Temperature + Flour Temperature + Friction Factor*) = Target Water Temperature

*If you're mixing by hand, the Friction Factor will be close to 0. If you're using a mixer, use the instructions on page 73 to determine the Friction Factor.

Weigh Your Ingredients.

Incorporate Ingredients: In a large bowl, mix together the white flour, whole wheat flour/high extraction/freshly milled flour, and yeast. Add the water and mix with your fingertips or a spoon until no dry bits remain.

Resting Period: Set aside, covered with a clean kitchen towel, for 20 minutes to 1 hour to hydrate the flour.

Incorporate the Salt: Uncover the bowl. Sprinkle over the salt and use your fingers to scissor pinch it into the dough. I use my thumb and first finger to work the salt in from one side of the dough to the next.

Knead: Once the salt is incorporated and dissolved, use four closed fingers, pinky to index, and mix using the Rubaud method: Secure the bowl with your nondominant hand. Scoop your hand under the far end of the dough, lift slightly, drop, and scoop again. Repeat the scooping/digging motion, turning the bowl slightly every four or five scoops. Mix until the dough comes together, becomes uniform, and tightens up, 5 to 7 minutes.

Bulk Ferment with Stretch and Folds: Transfer the dough to a clean, very lightly oiled plastic or glass bowl. Set aside, covered with plastic wrap or a clean kitchen towel, at room temperature for 30 minutes.

After 30 minutes, uncover the bowl. Place a small bowl of cold water next to the dough bowl. Stretch and fold the dough in the bowl to develop more strength. Every time you touch the dough, dip your hand in the water first. Starting at 12 o'clock, pull the quadrant of dough upward gently 6 to 12 inches (as much as the dough allows without tearing),

then press it gently onto itself. Turn the bowl a half turn and repeat. Next, turn the bowl a quarter turn and repeat the lifting/pressing, then a half turn and repeat. The dough will tighten up and get stronger during the series of stretch and folds. Set aside, covered with plastic wrap or a clean kitchen towel, at room temperature, for another 30 minutes.

Repeat the stretch and folds every 30 minutes. After 2 hours from the beginning of bulk fermentation, the dough should feel like there's a bit of gas building up in it, and it should pass the Window Pane Test (see page 75). Cover with plastic wrap and place in the refrigerator to rest overnight. If it feels like there's no gas production after 2 hours, set the bowl aside until the dough has increased in volume by at least 20 percent before transferring to the refrigerator. Overnight there will be a little more gas development.

DAY 2

The Next Morning (or at least 12 hours later), remove the bowl from the refrigerator and uncover. Stretch and fold the dough once more in the bowl. The dough will feel stronger. Cover with plastic wrap and return to the refrigerator.

Divide and Round: Before bed (or at least 12 hours later), remove the bowl from the refrigerator and uncover. Turn the dough out onto a lightly floured work surface, allowing it to gently release from the bowl. Handle the dough with extreme care. Using a dough scraper, cut the dough into seven equal pieces weighing about 255 grams each. If you are making a pan pie, cut the dough into two equal pieces weighing about 900 grams each.

Working with one piece of dough, bring the top half of the dough (from 12 o'clock) and lift and press it into the center of the dough. Next, bring the bottom half of the dough and lift and press it into the center. Take the left side of the dough and lift and press it into the center. Repeat with the right side. Then, take four corners and pull and fold them into the center of the ball and gently press to attach. Do not flatten. Be sure the ball is round and the bottom is sealed, pinching it closed if necessary. Gently flip the dough seam-side down. Repeat this process with the remaining dough pieces.

Place each ball into individual, very lightly oiled plastic containers large enough to allow each ball to double in volume. You can also place the balls in a lightly floured dough tray or baking sheet, dust their surface with flour, and cover with plastic wrap.

Proof: Transfer the dough to the refrigerator to rest overnight (or for at least 12 hours).

DAY 3

Bring the Dough to Room Temperature: The next day (or at least 12 hours later), 2 to 3 hours before stretching and baking, remove the dough from the refrigerator and set it aside to reach room temperature. The dough should have substantially increased in volume in the refrigerator. If it has not, allow it to increase in volume at room temperature before baking. The dough is ready when it has increased in volume by 20 percent and passes the Poke Test (springs back slowly and leaves a slight indentation when poked, page 89).

Preheat Your Oven: At least 1 hour before baking, preheat the oven to 500°F and set a baking stone or steel on a rack 6 to 8 inches below the top of the oven to preheat as well. You want the oven as hot as possible so turn the broiler on during the last 10 minutes if your oven allows. Turn off the broiler before you load the oven.

Stretch: Flour the top of a dough ball. If it is in a container, turn the dough out onto a generously floured surface. If it is in a dough tray or resting on a baking sheet, with your nondominant hand resting gently on top of the floured dough ball, use a dough scraper to scoop up the dough. Then invert the dough and gently land it on a generously floured surface. Try not to damage any of the structure at all, and be as minimally invasive as possible. Keep track of the "top" and "bottom" of the dough. The top of your future pizza is the one currently facing the countertop.

Using extremely gentle movements with flat fingertips spread, apply pressure on the dough at 10 and 2 o'clock. Lift your hands and reposition on the dough closer to you. Move from the top of the dough toward you, pressing downward and outward. Leave an inch along the rim that you don't touch at all.

Flip the dough over. The top of the future pizza is now facing upward. Continue stretching the dough, using the technique that works best for you. One approach is to leave the dough on the counter and, with one hand in the center, pull at 3, 6, 9, and 12 o'clock. Another is to scoop up the dough from

below with your palms facing the counter, then turn the dough, stretching and pulling it in increments with your knuckles. Be super gentle and don't be afraid to rely on gravity, a great stretcher of pizza dough. Regardless of your technique, stretch the dough until you get to a 10- to 11-inch diameter. You will stretch it to a 12-inch diameter on the peel.

If making a pan pie, shape and bake the dough according to the instructions on page 118.

Pause and Assess.

Transfer to the Peel: Dust the peel with coarse rice flour. Next, wipe your hands to remove any excess moisture. Gently scoop up the dough, sliding your hands beneath it, palms facing the work surface. Shake off any excess flour and transfer the dough to the floured peel. Using flattened and spread fingertips, palms facing upward from underneath, gently pull the dough until the disk reaches 12 inches in diameter. Be sure your hands are dry when you do this, otherwise the dough will stick to the peel.

Build: Add your desired toppings from a recipe in Part 4 (page 169).

Bake: Bake according to the method on page 111 at 500°F for 6 to 7 minutes.

Rest and Evaluate: Analyze the pizza according to the Pizza Evaluation Rubric (page xviii) and take notes so your next bake is even better.

Slice, Eat, and Enjoy!

Repeat with remaining dough balls, allowing your stone or steel to adequately recover between bakes.

Adapting Dough for High Temperature Ovens

 To modify the Yeasted Whole Wheat, High Extraction, or Freshly Milled Flour Dough for a high temperature oven, simply reduce the hydration to 70 percent. In other words, modify the final mix to use 700 grams of water instead of 780 grams. If using a wood fired oven, aim for dough balls weighing 250 to 270 grams. For smaller models of the tabletop high temperature ovens, which accommodate smaller pies, aim for 200-gram balls.

SOURDOUGH BAKING

Sourdough baking used to be an intimidating concept for many, but one of the few silver linings of the COVID-19 pandemic is that people took to it and became obsessed. I get it. It's something you can nurture and it becomes a part of your life in a really beautiful way. I like to think of sourdough starter like having a family pet, only with a lot less work and it makes pizza. I derive a lot of joy from creating new starters and feeding my existing ones. This ritual of regular flour and water feedings is something I look forward to every day. It's almost meditative. If you're new to sourdough baking, I hope you will give it a try. You'll immediately notice how much more flavor you can tease out of flour and water with this simple, ancient tradition.

MAKING AND MAINTAINING A STARTER

A starter is a leavening agent that must be active and thriving to work efficiently. There are lots of ways to make and maintain a starter, and I share mine with you here. (I highly recommend engaging with other bakers about their starter schedule and approaches. It's an incredible bonding moment and you learn so much having talks like this!)

To start, I mix equal parts freshly milled whole wheat flour (I always reach for organic) with body temperature water. The rich array of yeast, bacteria, and nutrients present in the flour will proliferate more quickly in warm water than in cold, and the aim is to cultivate a lively colony of microbes. Then I set the mixture aside. The next "feeding" (24 hours later) is done at a 1:1:1 ratio, equal parts of the existing starter seed, water, and flour. A starter made with whole wheat flour may take just 2 or 3 days of feedings to show signs of activity—bubbles on the surface and around the edges and the acidic aromas of fermentation. (A starter made with white flour may take 7 days or more.) The precise amount of time depends on the temperature of your kitchen (warmer temperatures favor faster fermentation) and how much yeast and bacteria are naturally present in the flour.

Once the starter is fully active—doubling in volume within 4 to 5 hours of feeding—aim to always feed the starter at the same time and at the same temperature. This will help create consistent results.

Freshly milled whole wheat flour

Water, at about body temperature (90 to 100°F)

In a small glass or plastic container large enough for the initial mixture to triple in volume, combine 25 grams flour and 25 grams water and mix until smooth. Mark the level of the mixture with tape or a rubber band on the outside of the container. Cover with a clean kitchen towel and allow the mixture to sit at room temperature for 24 hours.

After 24 hours have passed, discard all but 25 grams of the mixture, then add another 25 grams each of flour and water and mix well.

Repeat the discarding and feeding process daily until the mixture doubles in volume within 4 to 5 hours of feeding, indicating your starter is active and ready to bake with. This could take a week or two.

Once the starter is thriving you can keep it alive and active in a few ways, depending on your needs. If you bake daily, or at least weekly, feed the starter at a 1:10:10 ratio (1 part starter to 10 parts water and flour) every 12 to 24 hours. Return to the 1:1:1 ratio the day you plan to mix dough. Use the desired starter temperature formula in each sourdough recipe to calculate the exact water temperature you need for your feedings before each bake.

If you're taking a good long break from baking, more than a week off, put the starter in the refrigerator a few hours after a 1:10:10 feeding. Three days before you intend to bake, return the starter to room temperature and resume regular feedings at 1:10:10 based on your upcoming baking schedule. Return to the 1:1:1 ratio the day you plan to mix dough.

The morning you plan to mix, do your final starter feeding 4 to 5 hours before you start mixing based on the Final Starter Feeding box in each recipe. Mark the starter level on the container. The starter is ready to use when it has at least doubled in volume. Use any leftover starter as the seed for your next starter batch.

Starter's Life Cycle

Once an active starter is fed flour and water, it has a predictable life cycle. At first, you won't notice any activity; it's young and the yeast is not visibly active and the bacteria isn't yet creating lactic and acetic acid that you can smell. As the fermentation activity increases, more gas is produced and the starter will rise and increase in volume. When it's at its peak, it will have more than doubled in volume, have lots of visible bubbles, and smell complex with a touch of acidity.

When the starter passes its peak, it begins to collapse because the microorganisms have consumed most of the sugar in the mixture so they no longer have food to eat, and therefore stop producing the carbon dioxide that gives the starter its lift. Meanwhile, the acid produced in this phase breaks down the gluten. The yeast starts dying and the acids created by the bacteria will start to over-proliferate. The starter will begin to smell like vinegar and alcohol. If you use an overripe starter like this to make dough, the result will be flat and acidic, the crust won't rise or brown, and the crumb will be dense.

The key to starter maintenance is keeping the yeast population fed and the acid population in control. Managing timed feedings, staying on a schedule, and keeping the temperature constant are critical to a healthy starter in which the yeast and bacteria colonies are in balance. For me this means feeding daily at room temperature (twice daily if I plan on baking regularly, once in the morning and once at night).

If I forget to feed my starter for 2 days (I'm usually really good about it but two kids and a pizzeria can throw some wrenches in the works), I am left with a soupy, acidic mess. But all is not lost. I discard most of it and apply a 1:10:10 feeding (1 part starter, 10 parts each flour and water), which dramatically lowers the overall acidity of the mixture. I repeat this 1:10:10 feeding every 12 hours until the starter is more than doubling in volume. Once the starter is healthy again, it's ready to bake with.

SAME DAY SOURDOUGH

NAME YOUR INTENTION:
Manage the fermentation with sourdough starter, coax out incredible complex flavors through fermentation, produce a pizza that exhibits all the characteristics of the Pizza Evaluation Rubric, develop and bake off dough in a single day.

Once you've mastered the yeasted dough recipes, getting the results laid out in the Pizza Evaluation Rubric, you are ready for the incredible and infinitely fascinating world of naturally leavened dough. Sourdough baking, while more advanced than yeasted dough, doesn't have to be intimidating. On the contrary, it should be exciting to know that even beginner sourdough bakers can tap into flavors and aromas that just aren't feasible with commercial yeasts. You can make this a 1-day or 2-day recipe; the approaches yield slightly different flavors, aromas, and textures. Try both and compare. However, note that a 3- or 4-day fermentation will lead to too much acid building up in the dough.

Speaking of possibilities, there are infinite ways to prepare sourdough pizza. My approach here is to use 20 percent whole wheat, high extraction, or freshly milled flour, all of which come from the starter. If you're maintaining your starter based on the recipe on page 155, you're good to go. If you already have a

starter of your own and have been maintaining it with white flour, transition to whole wheat, high extraction, or freshly milled flour feedings beginning 3 days before mixing. You will also need to make sure the starter is very active before attempting this recipe. For the same day approach, mix in the morning so you can bake in the evening. Alternatively, you can make this a 2-day recipe. I provide a schedule for both scenarios.

Makes 4 balls weighing about 270 grams each for round pizza; or 1 ball weighing about 270 grams for round pizza and 1 ball weighing about 850 grams for pan pizza.

Desired dough temperature: 73°F

Percentage of pre-fermented flour (the percentage of the total flour weight that is present in the starter): 20 percent

INGREDIENTS	BAKER'S PERCENTAGES	TOTAL FORMULA
White flour	80%	500 grams
Whole wheat, high extraction, or freshly milled flour	20%	125 grams
Water	78%	490 grams
Fine sea salt	2%	13 grams
Total	180%	1128 grams

INGREDIENTS	FINAL MIX
White flour, plus more for dusting	500 grams
Water	365 grams
Starter	250 grams
Fine sea salt	13 grams
Extra-virgin olive oil, for oiling	
Rice flour, for dusting the peel	
Total	1128 grams

DAY 1

Final Starter Feeding: Feed the starter according to the box at right.

Calculate Target Water Temperature: Measure the room temperature and the temperature of the flour and starter and use the formula below to determine the water temperature:

(73°F x 4) – (Air Temperature + Flour Temperature + Starter Temperature + Friction Factor*) = Target Water Temperature (°F)

*If you're mixing by hand, the Friction Factor will be close to 0. If you're using a mixer, use the instructions on page 73 to determine the Friction Factor.

Weigh Your Ingredients.

Incorporate Ingredients: Once your starter has doubled in volume, mix together the white flour and water from the final mix with your fingertips or a spoon until no dry bits remain.

Autolyse: Set the mixture aside, covered with a clean kitchen towel, for 20 minutes to 1 hour to hydrate the flour (if you prefer, you can also mix the flour and water at the time you do your final starter feeding for an extended autolyse).

Incorporate the Starter: Add the starter to the flour mixture. Use four closed fingers, pinky to index, and mix using the Rubaud method: Secure the bowl with your nondominant hand. Scoop your hand under the far end of the dough, lift slightly, drop, and scoop again. Turn the bowl slightly every four or five scoops. Repeat the scooping/digging motion until the starter is fully incorporated.

Incorporate the Salt: Sprinkle over the salt and use your fingers to scissor pinch it into the dough. I use my thumb and first finger to work the salt in from one side of the dough to the next.

Knead: Once the salt is incorporated and dissolved, continue mixing using the Rubaud method for 5 to 7 minutes more.

Bulk Ferment with Stretch and Folds: Transfer the dough to a clean, very lightly oiled plastic or glass bowl. Set aside, covered with plastic wrap or a clean kitchen towel, at room temperature for 30 minutes.

After 30 minutes, uncover the bowl. Place a small bowl of cold water next to the dough bowl. Stretch and fold the dough in the bowl to develop more strength. Every time you touch the dough, dip your hand in the water first. Starting at 12 o'clock, pull the quadrant of dough upward gently 6 to 12 inches (as much as the dough allows without tearing), then press it gently onto itself. Turn the bowl a half turn and repeat. Next, turn the bowl a quarter turn and repeat the lifting/pressing, then a half turn and repeat. The dough will tighten up and get stronger during the series of stretch and folds. Set aside, covered with

Final Starter Feeding

Before you mix dough made with starter, the starter must be very active in order to properly ferment the dough. The final starter feeding is done 4 to 5 hours before mixing and produces enough starter for the final mix, plus excess, which becomes the seed for your next starter batch. Feed the excess. If you want to mix dough the following day, leave it out at room temperature. Otherwise, refrigerate it, then return to feeding it every 12 hours beginning 3 days before your next bake.

Desired starter temperature: 78°F
Makes 300 grams starter

> 100 grams starter
> 100 grams water
> 100 grams whole wheat, high extraction, or freshly milled flour

Use the desired starter temperature (78°F) to calculate the water temperature needed:

(78°F x 4) – (Air Temperature + Starter Temperature + Flour Temperature) = Target Water Temperature (°F)

Four to 5 hours before you plan to mix, combine the starter, water, and flour in a medium bowl and mix well. Set aside, covered, until at least doubled in volume and therefore very active.

plastic wrap or a clean kitchen towel, at room temperature, for another 30 minutes.

Repeat the stretch and folds every 30 minutes until the dough has increased in volume by about 20 percent and it passes the Window Pane Test (see page 75), 2 to 3 hours from the beginning of bulk fermentation.

Divide and Round: Turn the dough out onto a lightly floured work surface, allowing it to gently release from the bowl. Handle the dough with extreme care. Using a dough scraper, cut the dough into four equal pieces weighing about 270 grams each for round pizzas, or into two pieces with one ball weighing about 270 grams for one round pizza and one ball weighing about 850 grams for one pan pizza.

Working with one piece of dough, bring the top half of the dough (from 12 o'clock) and lift and press it into the center of the dough. Next, bring the bottom half of the dough and lift and press it into the center. Take the left side of the dough and lift and press it into the center. Repeat with the right side. Then, take four corners and pull and fold them into the center of the ball and gently press to attach. Do not flatten. Be sure the ball is round and the bottom is sealed, pinching it closed if necessary. Gently flip the dough seam-side down. Repeat this process with the remaining dough pieces.

Place each ball into individual, lightly oiled plastic containers large enough to allow each ball to double in volume. You can also place the balls in a lightly floured dough tray or baking sheet, dust their surface with flour, and cover with plastic wrap.

Proof: Set aside at room temperature if you intend to bake 3 to 4 hours later. Or transfer to the refrigerator to rest overnight (or up to 12 hours), but be sure to take the containers out of the refrigerator 2 to 3 hours before baking.

Determine When to Bake: The dough is ready when it has increased in volume by at least 50 percent and passes the Poke Test (springs back slowly and leaves a slight indentation when poked, page 89).

Preheat Your Oven: At least 1 hour before baking, preheat the oven to 500°F and set a baking stone or steel on a rack 6 to 8 inches below the top of the oven to preheat as well. Turn the broiler on during the last 10 minutes if your oven allows. Turn off the broiler before you load the oven.

Stretch: Flour the top of a dough ball. If it is in a container, turn the dough out onto a generously floured surface. If it is in a dough tray or resting on a baking sheet, with your nondominant hand resting gently on top of the floured dough ball, use a dough scraper to scoop up the dough. Then invert the dough and gently land it on a generously floured surface. Try not to damage any of the structure at all, and be as minimally invasive as possible. Keep track of the "top" and "bottom" of the dough. The top of your future pizza is the one currently facing the countertop.

Using extremely gentle movements with flat fingertips spread, apply pressure on the dough at 10 and 2 o'clock. Lift your hands and reposition on the dough closer to you. Move from the top of the dough toward you, pressing downward and outward. Leave an inch along the rim that you don't touch at all.

Flip the dough over. The top of the future pizza is now facing upward. Continue stretching the dough, using the technique that works best for you. One approach is to leave the dough on the counter and, with one hand in the center, pull at 3, 6, 9, and 12 o'clock. Another is to scoop up the dough from below with your palms facing the counter, then turn the dough, stretching and pulling it in increments with your knuckles. Be super gentle and don't be afraid to rely on gravity, a great stretcher of pizza dough. Regardless of your technique, stretch the dough until you get to a 10- to 11-inch diameter. You will stretch it to a 12-inch diameter on the peel.

If making a pan pie, shape and bake the dough according to the instructions on page 118.

Pause and Assess.

Transfer to the Peel: Dust the peel with coarse rice flour. Next, wipe your hands to remove any excess moisture. Gently scoop up the dough, sliding your hands beneath it, palms facing the work surface. Shake off any excess flour and transfer the dough to the floured peel. Using flattened and spread fingertips, palms facing upward from underneath, gently pull the dough until the disk reaches 12 inches in diameter. Be sure your hands are dry when you do this, otherwise the dough will stick to the peel.

Build: Add your desired toppings from a recipe in Part 4 (page 169).

Bake: Bake according to the method on page 111 at 500°F for 6 to 7 minutes.

Rest and Evaluate: Analyze the pizza according to the Pizza Evaluation Rubric (page xviii) and take notes so your next bake is even better.

Slice, Eat, and Enjoy!

Repeat with remaining dough balls, allowing your stone or steel to adequately recover between bakes.

Using a Mixer: Sourdough Recipes

For this and other starter-based recipes, if you choose to use a mechanical mixer, combine 85 percent of the water, flour, and starter. Mix until incorporated. Autolyse for 20 minutes to 1 hour. Slowly sprinkle in the salt while mixing. Bring the dough to medium gluten development (see page 74). Add the remaining water and mix until the water is fully absorbed. Set the dough aside, covered, for 1 hour, then do a stretch and fold to build a bit of additional strength. Set aside for 1 hour more, or until the dough has passed the Window Pane Test (see page 75) and has increased in volume by 20 percent, then follow the method at left from Divide and Round.

SAME DAY SOURDOUGH
FOR A HIGH TEMPERATURE OVEN

NAME YOUR INTENTION:
Manage the fermentation with sourdough starter, coax out incredible complex flavors through fermentation, dial in your wood fired or other high temperature oven settings to produce a pizza that exhibits all the desirable characteristics of the Pizza Evaluation Rubric.

Although similar in many ways to the home oven Same Day Sourdough, this dough has a lower hydration, which is specifically adapted to higher temperature ovens. Follow the method for a 12-inch pizza if you have a wood fired masonry oven or any high temperature oven that can accommodate a 12-inch pie, like the Ooni Koda 16. If your oven has a small opening and cooking surface like a Roccbox, stretch the dough to 10 inches instead of 12.

Makes 4 balls weighing about 275 grams each for 12-inch round pizzas; or 5 balls weighing about 220 grams each for 10-inch round pizzas

Desired dough temperature: 73°F

Percentage of pre-fermented flour (the percentage of the total flour weight that is present in the starter): 20 percent

INGREDIENTS	BAKER'S PERCENTAGES	TOTAL FORMULA
White flour	80%	518 grams
Whole wheat, high extraction, or freshly milled flour	20%	129 grams
Water	70%	453 grams
Fine sea salt	2%	13 grams
Total	172%	1113 grams

INGREDIENTS	FINAL MIX
White flour, plus more for dusting	518 grams
Water	324 grams
Starter	258 grams
Fine sea salt	13 grams
Extra-virgin olive oil, for oiling	
Rice flour, for dusting the peel	
Total	1113 grams

Final Starter Feeding

Before you mix dough made with starter, the starter must be very active and fed in advance of the mix. The final starter feeding is done 4 to 5 hours before mixing and produces enough starter for the final mix, plus excess, which becomes the seed for your next starter batch. Feed the excess. If you want to mix dough the following day, leave it out at room temperature. Otherwise, refrigerate it, then return to feeding it every 12 hours beginning 3 days before your next bake.

Desired starter temperature: 78°F
Makes 300 grams starter

100 grams starter
100 grams water
100 grams whole wheat, high extraction, or freshly milled flour

Use the desired starter temperature (78°F) to calculate the water temperature needed:

(78°F x 4) – (Air Temperature + Starter Temperature + Flour Temperature) = Target Water Temperature (°F)

Four to 5 hours before you plan to mix, combine the starter, water, and flour in a medium bowl and mix well. Set aside, covered, until at least doubled in volume.

Follow the Instructions for Same Day Sourdough (page 158). The only variations to keep in mind are:

Preheat your high temperature oven according to the wood fired baking instructions (page 124) or the manufacturer's manual, taking into consideration that preheating a wood fired oven could take up to 4 hours.

Shape the Dough into 10- or 12-inch pies depending on the size of your oven.

"CHOOSE YOUR OWN ADVENTURE" DOUGH

NAME YOUR INTENTION:

Hone your senses and dough intuition to determine proper hydration for your dough, manage fermentation with single variety wheat flour, execute a pizza that exhibits all the desirable characteristics of the Pizza Evaluation Rubric.

You've honed your skills with high hydration doughs with the recipes I have given you. Now it's your turn. Use what you have learned, choose a grain, and put your knowledge to work. After all that practice, this is the starting point of a real adventure. The sky's the limit and you can follow the journey anywhere your local grain availability or internet shopping cart take you.

This is the dough recipe that most closely resembles the spirit of the one we use at Razza. It really embodies what we do there: Seek inspiration from the raw materials we get from great mills. The journey of building relationships that introduce us to new flours is thrilling. And it's so much fun learning to use a new flour for the first time.

Another great thing about this dough is that it is incredibly flexible. It has a long window of usability, meaning I can start baking off pizzas at 5 p.m. and the dough is still going strong hours later—definitely not a given as some doughs rapidly overproof while on deck waiting to be baked.

Use any single variety wheat for this recipe as long as its protein quantity is between 11 and 13 percent. I love Cairnspring Mills' Yecora Rojo, which is a touch higher in protein but has incredible flavor. You can even blend several freshly milled wheats if you wish. Look for flour in the T70 (see page 9) or lower category so the bran doesn't inhibit gluten development. If whole wheat flour is all you have, sift out as much bran as you possibly can with a fine mesh sieve, weigh the sifted flour, and use the quantity required for the recipe below. Alternatively, you can blend the whole wheat flour with white flour.

This recipe is intended for advanced bakers who are more comfortable with visual and tactile cues

than strict schedules and timing. I give you a desired dough temperature to hit and visual and tactile indicators for when the dough is properly hydrated (this part really depends on the flour you choose, hence the hydration range noted in the recipe). Wetter doughs ferment slightly faster than less hydrated ones and fermentation rates depend on the flour you use, so the procedure focuses on visual cues instead of timing.

The dough is made with the double hydration technique (see page 66) in which most of the water is added in an initial stage; then, once the dough reaches medium gluten development, the remaining water is added in small increments. Depending on the flour, you may or may not need all of the water. This is where your intention, oven, and flour choice all come into play. Only use all of the water if you're making a pan pie (the bake requires extra hydration) or if the flour can absorb all of it.

Begin feeding your starter with the whole wheat, high extraction, or freshly milled flour of your choosing beginning 3 days before you intend to bake.

Results will vary depending on final hydration, but generally makes 6 balls weighing about 270 grams each for round pizza; or 2 balls weighing about 800 grams each for pan pizza

Desired dough temperature: 75°F

Percentage of pre-fermented flour (the percentage of the total flour weight that is present in the starter): 11 percent

INGREDIENTS	BAKER'S PERCENTAGES	TOTAL FORMULA
Single variety flour	100%	900 grams
Water	78 to 83%	700 to 750 grams
Fine sea salt	2%	18 grams
Total	180 to 185%	1618 to 1668 grams

INGREDIENTS	FINAL MIX
Single variety flour	800 grams
Water	600 to 650 grams
Starter	200 grams
Fine sea salt	18 grams
Extra-virgin olive oil, for oiling	
Rice flour, for dusting the peel	
Total	1618 to 1668 grams

DAY 1

Final Starter Feeding: Feed the starter according to the box at right.

Calculate Target Water Temperature: Measure the room temperature and the temperature of the flour and starter and use the formula to determine the target water temperature.

(75°F x 4) − (Air Temperature + Flour Temperature + Starter Temperature + Friction Factor*) = Target Water Temperature (°F)

*If you're mixing by hand, the Friction Factor will be close to 0. If you're using a mixer, use the instructions on page 73 to determine the Friction Factor.

Incorporate Ingredients: Once your starter has at least doubled in volume, mix together the flour and 600 grams of water from the final mix with your fingertips or a spoon until no dry bits remain.

Autolyse: Set the mixture aside, covered with a clean kitchen towel, for 20 minutes to 1 hour to hydrate the flour (if you prefer, you can also mix the flour and water at the time you do the final starter feeding for an extended autolyse).

Incorporate the Starter: Add the starter to the autolysed dough. Use four closed fingers, pinky to index, and mix using the Rubaud method: Secure

Final Starter Feeding

Before you mix dough made with starter, the starter must be very active and fed in advance of the mix. The final starter feeding is done 4 to 5 hours before mixing and produces enough starter for the final mix, plus excess, which becomes the seed for your next starter batch. Feed the excess. If you want to mix dough the following day, leave it out at room temperature. Otherwise, refrigerate it, then return to feeding it every 12 hours beginning 3 days before your next bake.

Use the flour you've chosen for this recipe to scale up and feed your starter.
Desired Starter Temperature: 78°F
Makes 300 grams starter

> 100 grams starter
> 100 grams water
> 100 grams whole wheat, whole
>   grain, or high extraction flour

Use the desired starter temperature (78°F) to calculate the water temperature needed:

(78°F x 4) − (Air Temperature + Starter Temperature + Flour Temperature) = Target Water Temperature (°F)

Four to 5 hours before you plan to mix, combine the starter, water, and flour in a medium bowl and mix well. Set aside, covered, until at least doubled in volume.

the bowl with your nondominant hand. Scoop your hand under the far end of the dough, lift slightly, drop, and scoop again. Turn the bowl slightly every four or five scoops. Repeat the scooping/digging motion until all the starter is incorporated.

Incorporate the Salt: Sprinkle over the salt and use your fingers to scissor pinch it into the dough. I use my thumb and first finger to work the salt in from one side of the dough to the next.

Knead: Once the salt is incorporated and dissolved, continue mixing using the Rubaud method for 5 to 7 minutes more. Use your senses to assess how wet or dry the dough is and how strong or weak it feels. That will determine if you need to add additional water. If the dough feels loose and wet, don't add any additional water and continue mixing until the dough tightens up. If the dough feels strong and dry or tough, add the remaining water 10 grams at a time, mixing until the dough feels supple and soft and tacky but not too sticky and some strength has developed. You may not need all the water.

Bulk Ferment with Stretch and Folds: Transfer the dough to a clean, lightly oiled plastic or glass bowl. Set aside, covered with plastic wrap or a clean kitchen towel, at room temperature for 20 minutes.

After 20 minutes, uncover the bowl. Place a small bowl of cold water next to the dough bowl. Stretch and fold the dough in the bowl to develop more strength. Every time you touch the dough, dip your hand in the water first. Starting at 12 o'clock, pull the quadrant of dough upward gently 6 to 12 inches (as much as the dough allows without tearing), then press it gently onto itself. Turn the bowl a half turn and repeat. Next, turn the bowl a quarter turn and repeat the lifting/pressing, then a half turn and repeat. The dough will tighten up and get stronger during the series of stretch and folds. Set aside, covered with plastic wrap or a clean kitchen towel, at room temperature, for another 20 minutes.

Repeat the stretch and folds every 20 minutes until the dough has increased in volume by about 20 percent and it passes the Window Pane Test (see page 75).

Divide and Round: Turn the dough out onto a lightly floured work surface, allowing it to gently release from the bowl. Handle the dough with extreme care. Using a dough scraper, cut the dough into six equal pieces weighing about 270 grams each for round pizza, or two balls weighing about 800 grams each for pan pizza.

Working with one piece of dough, bring the top half of the dough (from 12 o'clock) and lift and press it into the center of the dough. Next, bring the bottom half of the dough and lift and press it into the center. Take the left side of the dough and lift and press it into the center. Repeat with the right side. Then, take four corners and pull and fold them into the center of the ball and gently press to attach. Do not flatten. Be sure the ball is round and the bottom is sealed, pinching it closed if necessary. Gently flip the dough seam-side down. Repeat this process with the remaining dough pieces.

Place each ball into individual, very lightly oiled plastic containers large enough to allow each ball to double in volume. You can also place the balls in a lightly floured dough tray or baking sheet, dust their surface with flour, and cover with plastic wrap.

Proof: Transfer to the refrigerator to rest overnight.

DAY 2

Determine When to Bake: Remove the dough from the refrigerator 2 to 3 hours before baking. The dough is ready when it has increased in volume and when it passes the Poke Test (springs back slowly and leaves a slight indentation when poked, page 89).

Preheat Your Oven: At least 1 hour before baking, preheat the oven to 500°F and set a baking stone or steel on a rack 6 to 8 inches below the top of the oven to preheat as well. Turn the broiler on during the last 10 minutes if your oven allows. Turn off the broiler before you load the oven.

Stretch: Flour the top of a dough ball. If it is in a container, turn the dough out onto a generously floured surface. If it is in a dough tray or resting on a baking sheet, with your nondominant hand resting gently on top of the floured dough ball, use a dough scraper to scoop up the dough. Then invert the dough and gently land it on a generously floured surface. Try not to damage any of the structure at all, and be as minimally invasive as possible. Keep track of the "top" and "bottom" of the dough. The top of your future pizza is the one currently facing the countertop.

Using extremely gentle movements with flat fingertips spread, apply pressure on the dough at 10 and 2 o'clock. Lift your hands and reposition on the dough closer to you. Move from the top of the dough toward you, pressing downward and outward. Leave an inch along the rim that you don't touch at all.

Flip the dough over. The top of the future pizza is now facing upward. Continue stretching the dough, using the technique that works best for you. One approach is to leave the dough on the counter and, with one hand in the center, pull at 3, 6, 9, and 12 o'clock. Another is to scoop up the dough from below with your palms facing the counter, then turn the dough, stretching and pulling it in increments with your knuckles. Be super gentle and don't be afraid to rely on gravity, a great stretcher of pizza dough. Regardless of your technique, stretch the dough until you get to a 10- to 11-inch diameter. You will stretch it to a 12-inch diameter on the peel.

If making a pan pie, shape and bake the dough according to the instructions on page 118.

Pause and Assess.

Transfer to the Peel: Dust the peel with coarse rice flour. Next, wipe your hands to remove any excess moisture. Gently scoop up the dough, sliding your hands beneath it, palms facing the work surface. Shake off any excess flour and transfer the dough to the floured peel. Using flattened and spread fingertips, palms facing upward from underneath, gently pull the dough until the disk reaches 12 inches in diameter. Be sure your hands are dry when you do this, otherwise the dough will stick to the peel.

Build: Add your desired toppings from a recipe in Part 4 (page 169).

Bake: Bake according to the method on page 111 at 500°F for 6 to 7 minutes.

Rest and Evaluate: Analyze the pizza according to the Pizza Evaluation Rubric (page xviii) and take notes so your next bake is even better.

Slice, Eat, and Enjoy!

Repeat with remaining dough balls, allowing your stone or steel to adequately recover between bakes.

HIGH TEMPERATURE OVEN "CHOOSE YOUR OWN ADVENTURE" DOUGH

NAME YOUR INTENTION:
Hone your senses and dough intuition to determine proper hydration for your dough, manage fermentation with single variety wheat flour, dial in your high temperature oven skills to execute a pizza that exhibits all the desirable characteristics of the Pizza Evaluation Rubric, learn the delicate dance of managing your high temperature oven and naturally leavened dough.

To make dough for high temperature ovens, prepare your starter as you would for the home oven "Choose Your Own Adventure" recipe (page 164). This recipe is derived from that one but has a lower hydration (69 to 72 percent versus 78 to 83 percent). The desired dough temperature and desired starter temperature are the same as for the "Choose Your Own Adventure" Dough, 75°F and 78°F, respectively.

Makes 7 balls weighing about 215 grams each for 10-inch round pizzas; or 6 balls weighing about 250 grams each for 12-inch round pizzas.

Desired dough temperature: 75°F

Percentage of pre-fermented flour (the percentage of the total flour weight that is present in the starter): 11 percent

INGREDIENTS	BAKER'S PERCENTAGES	TOTAL FORMULA
Single variety flour	100%	900 grams
Water	69 to 72%	620 to 650 grams
Fine sea salt	2%	18 grams
Total	171 to 174%	1538 to 1568 grams

INGREDIENTS	FINAL MIX
Single variety flour	800 grams
Water	520 to 550 grams
Starter	200 grams
Fine sea salt	18 grams
Extra-virgin olive oil, for oiling	
Rice flour, for dusting the peel	
Total	1538 to 1568 grams

Follow the Instructions for home oven "Choose Your Own Adventure" (page 163). The only variations to keep in mind are:

Incorporate Ingredients: mix 520 grams of water with your fingertips or a spoon until no dry bits remain, the follow the remaining instructions.

Preheat your high temperature oven according to the wood fired baking instructions (page 124) or the manufacturer's manual, taking into consideration that preheating a wood fired oven could take up to 4 hours.

Shape the Dough into 10- or 12-inch pies depending on the size of your oven.

PART 4

CLASSIC AND SEASONAL PIZZAS, SAUCES, AND CONDIMENTS

Use any dough recipe from Part 3 to make the pizzas in this chapter. The toppings that follow are listed in the ideal ratio based on the Pizza Evaluation Rubric (page xviii) for 12-inch round pies. Scale them back slightly for 10-inch pies baked in small-mouthed high temperature ovens. Scale up by a factor of 2.25 for pan pies that bake in 16-inch square pans. Since the dimensions for pans vary wildly, you may need to dial in the exact proportion if your pan doesn't match precisely.

Speaking of dialing in, the suggested tomato sauce consistency may need to be adjusted—either strained to thicken or thinned with a bit of water—based on your observations of your Test Pie (see opposite). Similarly, bake your Test Pie with the recommended 1-inch pieces of mozzarella, changing the size if the cheese breaks or fails to flow. For some recipes like the Panna (page 199), in which mozzarella is a major protagonist, we also list a weight range (60 to 70 grams, for example). Use your Test Pie to determine what amount of mozzarella in that range you need for a successful distribution of toppings per the Pizza Evaluation Rubric.

When freestyling your own toppings, take into consideration what they contribute to the pizza (acidity, fat, and moisture, for example) and how their characteristics interact, keeping the produce guidelines from Part 1 and the pizza rubric in mind.

Test Pie

Pizza making is all about practice. Even after spending nearly half of my life obsessing over pizza, I still think of each bake as a learning opportunity. A useful approach for me has been to treat the first pie of every bake as a test run. I analyze it using the Pizza Evaluation Rubric and based on those observations, I can adjust the oven settings, tomato sauce thickness and quantity, and the size of the cheese, and fine-tune other details to improve the next pizza I make. Test Pies also let you reflect on the success of the dough and the fermentation, which can't be adjusted in the moment, but will signal where you can improve on your dough the next time you mix.

ROSSA
(TOMATO)

Makes 1 pizza

Dough for 1 round 12-inch pizza from any of the doughs in Part 3 (page 139)

Scant ½ cup High Moisture Tomato Sauce (page 243) or Fresh Tomato Sauce (page 244) in season

½ garlic clove

Fresh basil leaves

Coarse sea salt

Extra-virgin olive oil

Rossa, literally "red" in Italian, puts the tomato sauce front and center. There's no melty cheese or unctuous pepperoni to hide behind, so it's really important to use the best product you can. I cannot stress enough how critical it is that you taste tomatoes before you make sauce with them (there's a whole tasting guide in Part 1, page 20) so you are really showcasing the best of what nature provides. I always use high quality whole peeled tomatoes like domestic Bianco DiNapoli brand (available at Whole Foods), imported Gustarosso (available from Gustiamo), or exceptional in-season fresh tomatoes.

The Rossa is a popular vegan option at the restaurant but if you eat dairy, by all means hit the finished pizza with a flurry of finely grated cheese, such as Parmigiano-Reggiano, Pecorino Romano, or any other hard grating cheese you love. Use a truffle shaver or a sharp knife to slice the garlic 1 to 1.5 millimeters thick to ensure it cooks through. If you wish, use fresh oregano in place of the basil—or in addition to it!

Stretch the dough as outlined in the Techniques chapter. Transfer to a floured peel.

Spoon the tomato sauce evenly over the pizza dough to the edge of the raised border, then shave over the garlic, distributing evenly. Distribute the basil leaves evenly. Season with salt and drizzle with olive oil.

Bake as directed on page 111.

Drizzle with more olive oil and serve immediately.

When using basil, tear large leaves before putting them on the pizza. Leave small leaves whole.

MARGHERITA

Makes 1 pizza

Dough for 1 round 12-inch pizza from any of the doughs in Part 3 (page 139)

¼ cup Tomato Sauce (page 243)

75 to 80 grams fresh mozzarella, torn or cut into 1-inch pieces

Coarse sea salt

Extra-virgin olive oil

Fresh basil leaves

There's no better place to start your cheese-based pizza practice than with the classic Margherita. Not only is it incredibly delicious—the appeal of acidic tomato, savory mozzarella, and herbaceous basil is undeniable and if I had to stick to one pie for the rest of my life, this is it—it also lets you isolate the cheese, sauce, and the bake. We use the Margherita to dial in the size of our mozzarella pieces, the moisture of our sauce, and the temperature of our ovens. The classic Margherita is also the inspiration for other pies at Razza: our Jersey Margherita (page 177), by far our most popular variation, and the Burrata (page 178). It's a reminder that even if you just draw on the basics, the flavor potential is endless.

There's some debate among pizza makers about when to use basil on a Margherita. We put basil on after the bake because it's aromatic and we love that bright green color. All these wonderful aromas pop as soon as the basil hits the hot pizza. We think there's a place for charred herbs on pizza (Jersey Margherita, for example), but we're after freshness in this case.

Stretch the dough as outlined in the Techniques chapter. Transfer to a floured peel.

Spoon the tomato sauce over the pizza dough to the edge of the raised border, then distribute the mozzarella evenly. Season with salt and drizzle with olive oil.

Bake as directed on page 111.

Garnish with basil leaves and drizzle with more olive oil. Serve immediately.

Drizzle olive oil in a spiral motion, beginning at the edge of the pizza and ending in the center of your pie.

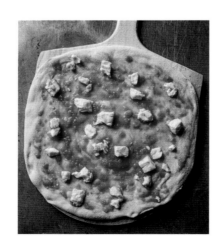

JERSEY MARGHERITA

Makes 1 pizza

Dough for 1 round 12-inch pizza from any of the doughs in Part 3 (page 139)

75 to 80 grams Jersey Girl fresh mozzarella, high quality domestic mozzarella di bufala, or high quality local and handmade mozzarella, torn or cut into 1-inch pieces

¼ cup Fresh Tomato Sauce (page 244) in season, or Low Moisture Tomato Sauce (page 243)

Fresh basil leaves

Coarse sea salt

Extra-virgin olive oil

This pie is one of Razza's variations on the classic Margherita (page 174) using all local products (hence the name) and cooking the basil on the pizza, rather than placing it on after baking. The Jersey Margherita is an expression of a time and a place. In the summer, we use fresh tomatoes to make the sauce, while the rest of the year we use Jersey Fresh canned whole peeled tomatoes, which taste like Jersey summer to me. Locally made Jersey Girl mozzarella and basil conspire with the tomatoes to give this pizza a real sense of terroir. I urge you to make this Margherita variation your own by using local products—I'd love to see a North Dakota Margherita, a Colorado Margherita, and a Georgia Margherita, all made by letting the location dictate the ingredients you use!

Jersey Girl mozzarella has a high fat and water content so we alternate drops of sauce between bits of cheese in order to regulate the rate of cheese flow. Cheese and sauce mingle together nicely and are punctuated with bits of charred basil.

Stretch the dough as outlined in the Techniques chapter. Transfer to a floured peel.

Distribute the mozzarella over the pizza dough, followed by drops of sauce between the cheese. Distribute the basil leaves, season with salt, and drizzle with olive oil.

Bake as directed on page 111.

Serve immediately drizzled with more olive oil.

BURRATA

Makes 1 pizza

Dough for 1 round 12-inch pizza from any of the doughs in Part 3 (page 139)

⅓ cup High Moisture Tomato Sauce (page 243) or Fresh Tomato Sauce (page 244) in season

½ garlic clove

Coarse sea salt

Extra-virgin olive oil

85 grams (3 ounces by weight) burrata, torn into bite sized pieces

Fresh basil leaves

The Burrata is our modern twist on the Margherita. It evokes the flavor combinations of that classic and gives us the same satisfying feeling of serving something incredibly simple with the building blocks of dairy, tomato, and basil. Burrata is luscious and decadent and begs for an acidic partner. Tomatoes provide a perfect flavor contrast and the texture of the tomato really shines here, too. If you like a super velvety and smooth tomato sauce, use a food mill with really fine mesh holes to crush the canned tomatoes to a pulp. If you like a chunkier texture, just use your hands. Thin slightly by mixing in a bit of water before spooning over the dough. You can also use a fresh tomato sauce instead of canned.

To ensure the garlic cooks fully, slice it super thin with a truffle shaver or sharp knife. Aim for 1 to 1.5 millimeters thick. The burrata goes on after cooking to preserve the texture of the curds and ensure that the cream remains sweetly lactic. It also provides a fun temperature contrast that really takes my brain on an adventure. The hot crust and sauce with room temperature burrata are a few of my favorite things.

Stretch the dough as outlined in the Techniques chapter. Transfer to a floured peel.

Spoon the tomato sauce evenly over the pizza dough to the edge of the raised border, then shave over the garlic, distributing evenly. Season with salt and drizzle with olive oil.

Bake as directed on page 111.

Distribute the burrata in drops evenly over the pizza. Garnish with basil leaves and drizzle with more olive oil. Serve immediately.

CORN PIE

Makes 1 pizza

Dough for 1 round 12-inch pizza from any of the doughs in Part 3 (page 139)

90 grams fresh mozzarella, torn or cut into 1-inch pieces

10 grams scamorza, grated

Kernels from 1 in-season corn cob (cob blanched until tender, kernels removed), about ½ cup

2 tablespoons Caramelized Onions (page 223)

Fermented Chili Sauce (page 248) to taste, in drops

Coarse sea salt

Extra-virgin olive oil

New Jersey summer produce has a brief and intense season and corn is one of the best products the state has to offer. Corn's sweetness pairs perfectly with savory cheeses like scamorza. Lately we've been using scamorza alongside fresh mozzarella to support our local Jersey Girl Cheese, which makes it, and it's been a huge hit. You can find scamorza in Italian delis and some supermarkets.

I admit the first time I saw corn on a pizza during a trip to Japan in 2006 I was a bit skeptical. I filed the memory in the back of my mind, and it returned during a particularly good Jersey corn season. At Razza we experimented with preparing the corn in different ways and settled on blanching as the best way to enhance its texture. The pizza became the most popular seasonal pie we do all year.

If you can't get scamorza, ricotta salata makes an equally pleasant salty counterpoint to the corn. We like to add a bit of acidity and heat to the pizza to contrast the sweetness of the corn in the form of the Fermented Chili Sauce, but if you prefer something that's not so spicy, harissa is a great substitute.

Stretch the dough as outlined in the Techniques chapter. Transfer to a floured peel.

Distribute the mozzarella, scamorza, corn, and onions evenly to the edge of the raised border, followed by dollops of chili sauce. Season with salt and drizzle with olive oil.

Bake as directed on page 111.

Drizzle with more olive oil and serve immediately.

FUNGHI (MUSHROOM)

Makes 1 pizza

Dough for 1 round 12-inch pizza from any of the doughs in Part 3 (page 139)

90 grams fresh mozzarella, torn or cut into 1-inch pieces

½ cup Roasted Mushrooms (page 185)

2 tablespoons Caramelized Onions (page 223)

10 grams scamorza, grated

Coarse sea salt

1 tablespoon finely chopped chives

Freshly grated Parmigiano-Reggiano

Funghi is our catch-all mushroom pizza and stays on the menu virtually year-round. Use the best in-season mushrooms you can reasonably afford, sourced locally if possible. We like single varieties like maitake (when we can get super fresh ones), but we also love mixing the textures of pioppini and cremini. If you're splashing out, get chanterelles and morels.

Depending on the season, we use herbs to complement the mushrooms' flavor. Feel free to tailor the herbal component to what you have and what you like. The recipe below calls for chives added after baking, but you can use minced rosemary (before the bake) or the leaves from 1 sprig of fresh thyme (after the bake) instead. A mix of herbs like thyme, rosemary, parsley, and lavender works great, too. Put them on after the bake.

Stretch the dough as outlined in the Techniques chapter. Transfer to a floured peel.

Distribute the mozzarella, mushrooms, onions, and scamorza evenly to the edge of the raised border. Season with salt.

Bake as directed on page 111.

Sprinkle with chives and a dusting of Parmigiano-Reggiano. Serve immediately.

(Continued)

ROASTED MUSHROOMS

Makes 2 cups (315 grams or ⅔ pound)

INGREDIENT	COOK'S PERCENTAGES
Mushrooms	100%
Salt	1%
Sherry vinegar	0.5%

1 pound mushrooms, torn or cut into bite sized pieces (I like porcini, maitake, cremini, chanterelles, and morels)

Extra-virgin olive oil

1% salt by weight (after roasting)

0.5% sherry vinegar by weight (after roasting)

You only need ½ cup of mushrooms for the Funghi and ¼ cup for the Bosco (page 213), but we recommend roasting a larger quantity so you have leftovers: add some herbs and serve them as a side dish or fold them into a frittata.

Preheat the oven to 425°F.

Distribute the mushrooms over a half-sheet pan and drizzle with olive oil to coat. Roast just until they start to caramelize, 15 to 20 minutes. Weigh the roasted mushrooms and season with 1 percent salt and 0.5 percent sherry vinegar by weight. The mushrooms will keep in a sealed container in the refrigerator for 3 days.

Cook's Percentages

I apply a similar concept of Baker's Percentages (see page 142) to some of the toppings and condiments like the Roasted Mushrooms here, Roasted Asparagus (page 192), and Fermented Chili Sauce (page 248). The main ingredient (roasted mushrooms, roasted asparagus, and chilis, for example) is treated as 100 percent of the recipe. The quantity of salt and other ingredients is then determined by weighing the main ingredient and calculating the quantity based on the exact percentage listed in the recipe, leading the main ingredients to be seasoned or to ferment predictably every time. Olive oil is excluded from the percentages because the amount you need depends on the surface area of your ingredients, which will vary.

ZUCCHINE (SUMMER SQUASH)

Makes 1 pizza

Dough for 1 round 12-inch pizza from any of the doughs in Part 3 (page 139)

100 grams fresh mozzarella, torn or cut into 1-inch pieces

80 grams (½ cup) Seasoned Squash (recipe follows)

Coarse sea salt

Extra-virgin olive oil

50 grams (¼ cup) high quality ricotta

Freshly ground black pepper

Lemon wedge

For this pizza you can theoretically use any variety of squash you like, but we stick to ones on the smaller side and roughly cylindrical (rather than crookneck) so all the slices are consistent. We also favor young squash. Once they get too big, the seeds start to take over and they bring an unpleasant texture. Speaking of texture, you absolutely must salt the squash in advance to reduce moisture and ensure the squash cooks properly and melts into the pizza.

Squash is one of the hardest toppings to pull off because its flavor is so delicate and it contains a lot of water so it has to be treated properly for the flavor to come through. To compensate for squash's low acidity, we serve this pizza with a lemon wedge in the middle and squeeze it over before slicing.

Stretch the dough as outlined in the Techniques chapter. Transfer to a floured peel.

Distribute the mozzarella and squash evenly to the edge of the raised border. Season with salt and drizzle with olive oil.

Bake as directed on page 111.

Distribute the ricotta evenly in dollops. Season with black pepper and drizzle with more olive oil.

Serve immediately with a lemon wedge in the middle.

(Continued)

SEASONED SQUASH

INGREDIENT	COOK'S PERCENTAGES
Zucchini	100%
Salt	0.75%

2 medium (about 340 grams or ¾ pound) zucchini, sliced on a mandoline to 1 to 2 millimeters thick

0.75% salt by weight

Extra-virgin olive oil

Use squash of the same size but different colors to ensure consistency and to deliver a pleasing color contrast, respectively.

Weigh the zucchini and combine with 0.75 percent salt by weight in a medium bowl. Set aside, covered, in the refrigerator overnight. Drain and squeeze off any excess water, then drizzle with olive oil.

SPRING PIE

Makes 1 pizza

Dough for 1 round 12-inch pizza from any of the doughs in Part 3 (page 139)

75 to 80 grams fresh mozzarella, torn or cut into 1-inch pieces

½ cup (1 recipe) Roasted Asparagus (recipe follows)

Sea salt

Extra-virgin olive oil

2 tablespoons Spring Pesto (page 251)

Freshly grated Parmigiano-Reggiano

Lemon wedge

Spring in New Jersey bursts onto the scene with warming sunshine after a long winter, bringing incredible new produce along with it. From late November until April, we don't get much fresh produce, mainly root vegetables like beets and potatoes. As great as they are, by March we're over them. Receiving the first fresh vegetables when the weather starts to warm up is extraordinarily exciting. All of a sudden, flowers are in bloom and the first warm days bring lots of herbs, greens, and the first asparagus. This pizza is an homage to that thrilling moment that ushers in the Garden State's growing season. The asparagus is roasted to bring out its caramelized flavors and the spritz of lemon brightens everything up. Ideally, you would make this pizza in season when the asparagus is tender and before the stems turn woody and become difficult to chew through.

Stretch the dough as outlined in the Techniques chapter. Transfer to a floured peel.

Distribute the mozzarella and asparagus evenly to the edge of the raised border. Season with salt and drizzle with olive oil.

Bake as directed on page 111.

Drizzle over the pesto and dust with Parmigiano-Reggiano.

Serve immediately with a lemon wedge in the middle.

(Continued)

ROASTED ASPARAGUS

Makes ½ cup

INGREDIENT	COOK'S PERCENTAGES
Asparagus	100%
Salt	1%

75 grams asparagus, sliced into 3- to 5-millimeter-thick coins

Extra-virgin olive oil

1% salt by weight (after roasting)

This recipe is best when the asparagus is very young and tender. Cut off the bottoms of the asparagus stalks when they become fibrous later in the season. Taste them raw to test. You can also just peel the bottom two-thirds of the stalk so it is the same thickness and a similar consistency as the tip. This shouldn't be necessary for very young asparagus. Be sure to wash the asparagus well. They thrive in sandy soil and may be gritty.

Preheat the oven to 450°F.

Drizzle the asparagus with enough olive oil to coat and roast on a half-sheet pan until they begin to take color, 10 to 15 minutes.

Weigh the roasted asparagus and season with 1 percent salt by weight.

PEA PIE

Dough for 1 round 12-inch pizza from any of the doughs in Part 3 (page 139)

110 grams fresh mozzarella, torn or cut into 1-inch pieces

½ cup shelled peas

30 grams (about 6 slices) guanciale, cut into 0.8-millimeter-thick pieces, torn

8 to 10 cloves Garlic Confit (page 249)

Freshly grated Parmigiano-Reggiano

This is one of those pies that Razza servers are most excited to talk about with diners. Most of our guests don't come in thinking they want peas on a pizza, but we only use fresh peas in season and they are glorious. It's worth spending all that time shucking fresh peas for such a sweet payoff. They're nothing like their frozen or out of season counterparts and have such beautiful flavor and firm texture. To make this a vegetarian pie, simply omit the guanciale. Replace it with dollops of high quality fresh ricotta if you'd like.

Stretch the dough as outlined in the Techniques chapter. Transfer to a floured peel.

Distribute the mozzarella, peas, guanciale, and garlic confit evenly to the edge of the raised border.

Bake as directed on page 111.

Serve immediately dusted with Parmigiano-Reggiano.

PROJECT HAZELNUT

Makes 1 pizza

Dough for 1 round 12-inch pizza from any of the doughs in Part 3 (page 139)

120 grams fresh mozzarella, torn or cut into 1-inch pieces

25 grams (¼ cup) raw hazelnuts, soaked in advance (see tip)

50 grams (¼ cup) high quality fresh ricotta

Coarse sea salt

Extra-virgin olive oil

1 teaspoon local honey

Over the years this has become one of the signature pies at Razza. Guests are always surprised to find hazelnuts on a pizza, much less locally grown ones. But they love it and not just because it's the product of this wonderful partnership we have with Rutgers University's Hazelnut Project (see page 49). It's so delicious and the rich fat and flavor of the nuts pair wonderfully with a little swirl of honey. The hazelnuts' texture is extraordinary and unlike any other I have encountered.

Stretch the dough as outlined in the Techniques chapter. Transfer to a floured peel.

Distribute the mozzarella, hazelnuts, and dollops of ricotta evenly to the edge of the raised border. Season with salt and drizzle with olive oil.

Bake as directed on page 111.

Drizzle with honey. Serve immediately.

> Gently heat up the honey to make it more pourable: Put a squeeze bottle of honey in a bowl of hot water like you would heat a baby's bottle.

Prepare the Hazelnuts

Place the hazelnuts in a medium bowl and pour over very hot (185 to 195°F) water to cover. Soak for 2 minutes, then drain. Alternatively, use the hottest water out of your faucet and soak the hazelnuts for 30 minutes, then drain.

PANNA (CREAM)

Makes 1 pizza

Dough for 1 round 12-inch pizza from any of the doughs in Part 3 (page 139)

¼ cup Tomato Sauce (page 243)

60 to 70 grams fresh mozzarella, torn or cut into 1-inch pieces

1 tablespoon heavy cream

Coarse sea salt

2 cups loosely packed arugula

Freshly grated Parmigiano-Reggiano

Our Panna is a variation on a Margherita, but instead of drizzling extra-virgin olive oil on it, we drizzle over an incredibly rich cow's cream from a dairy in Pennsylvania. When the cream mixes with the tomato it makes a kind of swirly pink penne alla vodka thing and it's great. The arugula is a wonderful peppery partner to the cream and tomato sauce. Use the best quality cream you can find. Often when I challenge myself to source a product that's better than what I can find at the supermarket, I make exciting discoveries. Who knows, the search for high quality cream may lead you to a fabulous local dairy.

Stretch the dough as outlined in the Techniques chapter. Transfer to a floured peel.

Spoon the tomato sauce over the pizza dough to the edge of the raised border, then distribute the mozzarella evenly. Drizzle over the heavy cream. Season with salt.

Bake as directed on page 111.

Distribute the arugula evenly over the pizza, then shave over Parmigiano-Reggiano and serve immediately.

PEPPERONI

Makes 1 pizza

Dough for 1 round 12-inch pizza from any of the doughs in Part 3 (page 139)

Scant ¼ cup Tomato Sauce (page 243)

70 to 75 grams fresh mozzarella, torn or cut into 1-inch pieces

40 grams pepperoni, cut into 1.75- to 2-millimeter-thick slices (about 24 slices)

½ garlic clove

Pepperoni pizza is an American classic and one of our most popular pies at Razza. The quality of pepperoni varies wildly, so seek out one that is as natural and artisanal as possible—insist on natural casing in particular. Read the label and stay away from the brands with loads of chemical additives. If you buy pre-sliced pepperoni, look for a thicker slice. Otherwise, buy a stick and use a sharp, heavy chef's knife to cut it 1.75 to 2 millimeters thick. The pepperoni will shrink as it cooks, curling around the edges to form cups that hold a pleasant pool of fat.

Stretch the dough as outlined in the Techniques chapter. Transfer to a floured peel.

Spoon the tomato sauce evenly over the pizza dough to the edge of the raised border. Distribute the mozzarella and pepperoni evenly, then shave over the garlic to a thickness of 1 to 1.5 millimeters using a truffle shaver or sharp knife.

Bake as directed on page 111.

Serve immediately.

GUANCIA

Makes 1 pizza

Dough for 1 round 12-inch pizza from any of the doughs in Part 3 (page 139)

Scant ¼ cup Tomato Sauce (page 243)

75 to 80 grams fresh mozzarella, torn or cut into 1-inch pieces

2 tablespoons shaved onion (1 to 2 millimeters thick)

30 grams (about 6 slices) guanciale, cut into 0.8-millimeter-thick pieces

Freshly grated Pecorino Romano

The *guancia* (cheek) pizza is named for guanciale (salt-cured pork jowl), a popular component in Roman cooking. The thickness of the guanciale you use really counts here; if it's too thin it will melt into the pizza; if it's too thick, it won't cook properly and will be hard to chew through. Going too thin is better than too thick. Staying with the Roman theme, we dust the baked pizza with Pecorino Romano, a salted sheep's milk cheese popular in the cuisine of the Italian capital.

Stretch the dough as outlined in the Techniques chapter. Transfer to a floured peel.

Spoon the tomato sauce evenly over the pizza dough to the edge of the raised border. Distribute the mozzarella, onion, and guanciale evenly.

Bake as directed on page 111.

Serve immediately dusted with Pecorino Romano.

To cut the guanciale easily without a deli slicer, place it in the freezer for 20 minutes. It will harden and be easier to slice.

DI NATALE

Makes 1 pizza

Dough for 1 round 12-inch pizza from any of the doughs in Part 3 (page 139)

¼ cup Tomato Sauce (page 243)

75 grams fresh mozzarella, torn or cut into 1-inch pieces

2 tablespoons roughly chopped, pitted, and rinsed black olives

1 tablespoon pine nuts

1 tablespoon raisins soaked in hot water for 10 minutes, or in cold water overnight, drained

½ garlic clove

Extra-virgin olive oil

Fresh basil leaves (optional)

Chili Oil (page 247)

In 2017, my friend and coauthor Katie Parla took me and my friends Nick and Cameron on an epic pizza tour of Campania. Of course we ate our weight in pizza, but we made many other stops along the way, including a place Katie loves in Sant'Anastasia called 'E Curti. At this historic trattoria near Naples, they serve a dish called sicchie d'a munnezza, which means "trash can," referring to the fact that it is made with cooking scraps that a Neapolitan family would have left over after preparing a Christmas (Natale) meal: tomato sauce, olives, pine nuts, raisins, garlic, and chilis. Neapolitans quickly cook these ingredients together, then toss with spaghetti. We instantly fell in love with this combination and introduced it as a pizza topping as soon as we returned. At the restaurant we serve the Di Natale with fresh basil leaves added after the bake. You can do so as well, in season. Use the best raisins that you can find. You can use a range of olives like Nicoise, Taggiasca, or any small black olive except for low quality or canned.

Stretch the dough as outlined in the Techniques chapter. Transfer to a floured peel.

Spoon the tomato sauce evenly over the pizza dough to the edge of the raised border. Distribute the mozzarella, olives, pine nuts, and raisins evenly. Shave over the garlic with a truffle shaver or sharp knife to 1 to 2 millimeters thick. Drizzle with olive oil.

Bake as directed on page 111.

Serve immediately, garnished with basil, if using, and drizzled with chili oil.

MONTAGNA

Dough for 1 round 12-inch pizza from any of the doughs in Part 3 (page 139)

¼ cup Tomato Sauce (page 243)

75 to 80 grams fresh mozzarella, torn or cut into 1-inch pieces

Coarse sea salt

Extra-virgin olive oil

25 grams (2 cups) loosely packed arugula

Parmigiano-Reggiano

30 grams (1 ounce) thinly sliced speck or prosciutto, torn

Montagna means "mountain" in Italian. Every time I am up in the Italian Alps I spend half the time plotting ways to stay. This pizza brings me right back there. It's not quite a substitute for the fresh mountain air and spectacular terrain of Alto Adige and Valle d'Aosta, but the juniper-scented speck brings a beautiful smoky and herbaceous flavor with a hint of sweetness. The speck should be sliced paper thin on a deli slicer—or you can omit it to make the Montagna vegetarian. Also feel free to substitute Piave or another hard grating cheese for the Parmigiano-Reggiano.

Stretch the dough as outlined in the Techniques chapter. Transfer to a floured peel.

Spoon the tomato sauce over the pizza dough to the edge of the raised border, then distribute the mozzarella evenly. Season with salt and drizzle with olive oil.

Bake as directed on page 111.

Distribute the arugula, then use a vegetable peeler to shave curls of Parmigiano-Reggiano directly over the pie. Drape over the speck. Drizzle with more olive oil. Serve immediately.

BIANCA

Dough for 1 round 12-inch pizza from any of the doughs in Part 3 (page 139)

120 grams fresh mozzarella, torn or cut into 1-inch pieces

Coarse sea salt

Extra-virgin olive oil or a splash of heavy cream

50 grams (¼ cup) high quality ricotta

Freshly grated Parmigiano-Reggiano

When I was a kid, my mom would often order a white (*bianca* in Italian) pie when we went out for pizza. I wasn't really into it because I didn't like the ricotta component. I suspect this had something to do with the watery, grainy, characterless ricotta that circulated in New Jersey in the '80s. I have changed my mind about ricotta since meeting wonderful local dairy farmers and getting to know their amazing products. The Bianca takes the classic white pizza and elevates it with quality dairy. If you have really good ricotta, it's a shame to cook it, so we typically put it on after the bake—making this pie diverge from the classic Jersey white pie in one more respect. You can even substitute the olive oil with a drizzle of luscious heavy cream if you wish.

Stretch the dough as outlined in the Techniques chapter. Transfer to a floured peel.

Distribute the mozzarella evenly. Season with salt and drizzle with olive oil.

Bake as directed on page 111.

Distribute dollops of ricotta evenly and sprinkle over the Parmigiano-Reggiano. Serve immediately.

SANTO

Makes 1 pizza

Dough for 1 round 12-inch pizza from any of the doughs in Part 3 (page 139)

Scant ¼ cup Tomato Sauce (page 243)

70 to 75 grams fresh mozzarella, torn or cut into 1-inch pieces

12 slivers very thinly sliced (1 to 2 millimeters thick) halved red onion

55 grams (2 ounces or ¼ cup) raw Sausage Mix (recipe below)

Chili Oil (page 247)

The Santo is one of the original Razza pies. My friend Cameron, whose family is from Calabria, loved talking about his trips there during which he would drizzle *olio santo* (literally "holy oil," Calabrian chili oil) over everything. I love to picture him in his ancestral homeland reveling in the region's penchant for heat, then returning to spread the spice gospel in New Jersey. The raw sausage, a nod to Calabria's love of pork, cooks beautifully during the bake and its caramelized exterior gives way to a tender pink middle.

Stretch the dough as outlined in the Techniques chapter. Transfer to a floured peel.

Spoon the tomato sauce over the pizza dough to the edge of the raised border, then distribute the mozzarella, onion, and sausage evenly.

Bake as directed on page 111.

Drizzle with chili oil and serve immediately.

SAUSAGE MIX

Makes 1 pound

About 450 grams (1 pound) raw ground pork

6 grams toasted fennel seeds

5 grams kosher salt

Pinch of crushed red pepper (optional)

1 garlic clove, minced

This recipe makes enough sausage for eight pies, so use any left over to make tomato sauce or breakfast sausage. Or stir in a raw egg and make sausage meatballs.

In a large bowl, combine the pork, fennel seeds, salt, red pepper, and garlic. The mixture will keep in the refrigerator for up to 1 day.

BOSCO

Dough for 1 round 12-inch pizza from any of the doughs in Part 3 (page 139)

3 tablespoons Tomato Sauce (page 243)

60 grams fresh mozzarella, torn or cut into 1-inch pieces

30 grams fontina cheese, cut into 1-centimeter cubes

¼ cup Roasted Mushrooms (page 185)

Coarse sea salt

Extra-virgin olive oil

1 grate of whole nutmeg

Mushrooms are one of my favorite things in the world. There's just something magical about them: They are ethereal and elusive to find in the wild, and they can communicate with one another using their mycelium structure. They are amazing and I am obsessed. We know so little about the vast and amazing fungi kingdom, so I'm always looking for new mushrooms to get a little bit closer to understanding this complex ingredient. If that's your thing, too, seek them out. At Razza, we're lucky enough to work with a forager named Dan Lipow of The Foraged Feast. He's our mushroom guy and all-around forest (*bosco* in Italian) guru.

This pizza is inspired by my walks in the woods with Dan. It was on those foraging trips looking for mushrooms that he taught me about Japanese knotweed, garlic mustard, and the whole range of local edible weeds. When I was growing up near these woods I had no idea there were all these amazing things growing there, only making my interest in the mushroom-filled forest more intense. Use any exciting seasonal mushrooms you can find, as long as you pre-roast them. Use the nutmeg very sparingly. You want just the faintest hint.

Stretch the dough as outlined in the Techniques chapter. Transfer to a floured peel.

Distribute drops of tomato sauce over the pizza dough followed by mozzarella between the sauce. Distribute the fontina and mushrooms evenly. Season with salt and drizzle with olive oil.

Bake as directed on page 111.

Grate over the nutmeg and serve immediately.

PUMPKIN PIE (OR WINTER SQUASH)

Makes 1 pizza

Dough for 1 round 12-inch pizza from any of the doughs in Part 3 (page 139)

100 grams fresh mozzarella, torn or cut into 1-inch pieces

½ cup Roasted Pumpkin (page 217)

¼ cup Caramelized Onions (page 223)

Coarse sea salt

Extra-virgin olive oil

2 tablespoons Homemade Breadcrumbs (page 217)

Freshly grated ricotta salata

1 grate of whole nutmeg

We wait as long as humanly possible to put the pumpkin pie on the menu at Razza because it signals the beginning of a long winter. It's not that we don't love pumpkin—we do!—but its arrival means a farewell to the diversity of warmer months. The silver lining is that because New Jersey grows so many fantastic heirloom pumpkin and squash varieties, we can get creative and change it up when a farmer brings us a new type.

The sweetness of the pumpkin is front and center here but the ricotta salata shines through, too, lending a wonderful salty component. We finish the pizza with breadcrumbs for a textural contrast with a practical function—we bake our bread at the restaurant and we're always looking for ways to use the small amounts we have left over. This pizza is pretty versatile so you can swap out the mozzarella for any good melter (I especially love Swiss cheeses) and the ricotta salata for any good hard grating cheese.

Stretch the dough as outlined in the Techniques chapter. Transfer to a floured peel.

Distribute the mozzarella, pumpkin, and onions evenly to the edge of the raised border. Season with salt and drizzle with olive oil.

Bake as directed on page 111.

Dust with breadcrumbs and the ricotta salata. Grate over the nutmeg and serve immediately.

(Continued)

ROASTED PUMPKIN

Makes 2 to 3 cups

INGREDIENT	COOK'S PERCENTAGES
Heirloom pumpkin	100%
Salt	1%

1 (approximately 2-pound) heirloom pumpkin or winter squash, peeled, seeds removed, and cut into ½-inch cubes

Extra-virgin olive oil

1% salt by weight

Use any pumpkin or winter squash, as long as they are easy to peel. Some of my favorites are Blue Hubbard, Delicata, and Honeynut. Seek out obscure varieties that grow near you and roast them to tease out beautiful sweet, caramelized flavors.

Preheat the oven to 425°F.

Combine the pumpkin with enough olive oil to coat on a half-sheet pan and roast for 40 minutes, until it pierces easily with a knife and just starts to brown. Weigh the pumpkin and season with 1 percent salt by weight. Cool completely. The roasted pumpkin will keep in a sealed container in the refrigerator for 3 days.

HOMEMADE BREADCRUMBS

Makes ½ cup

4 slices day-old bread, crusts cut off, cut into 1-inch cubes, and left out overnight to turn stale

Extra-virgin olive oil

2 fresh sage leaves

1 sprig fresh thyme, leaves picked

Preheat the oven to 250°F.

Combine the bread cubes and enough olive oil to coat and spread over a half-sheet pan. Toast until very crispy, about 20 minutes.

Transfer the cubes to a food processor and pulse with the sage and thyme until they are the consistency of coarse coffee grounds. The breadcrumbs will keep in a sealed container at room temperature for 2 weeks.

CAVOLINI (BRUSSELS SPROUTS)

Makes 1 pizza

Dough for 1 round 12-inch pizza from any of the doughs in Part 3 (page 139)

90 grams fresh mozzarella, torn or cut into 1-inch pieces

10 grams scamorza, grated

1 cup medium Brussels sprouts, outer leaves peeled, insides shaved into 1- to 2-millimeter-thick slices

1 tablespoon Melted Anchovies (page 221)

Freshly grated Parmigiano-Reggiano

I grew up in the 1980s and early 1990s, before Brussels sprouts had their moment, so initially I wasn't a huge fan—until my cousin Kevin came home from culinary school one year and cooked them for Thanksgiving dinner. He thinly shaved them and sweated them in a pan, teasing out all these amazing flavors. I was converted instantly. At the restaurant, we pick off the outer leaves and leave them whole, but shred the heart because the interior portion needs to break down a little bit more to cook at the same rate as the outer leaves.

The melted anchovies with garlic conjure fond memories of a trip to Piedmont, where a similar elixir, called *bagna cauda,* is served with crudités. It's a wonderful complement to the Brussels sprouts. You can use Garlic Confit (see page 249) as a substitute for the anchovies to make this pie vegetarian.

Stretch the dough as outlined in the Techniques chapter. Transfer to a floured peel.

Distribute the mozzarella over the pizza dough to the edge of the raised border followed by the scamorza and Brussels sprouts. Drizzle over the melted anchovies.

Bake as directed on page 111.

Serve immediately, dusted with Parmigiano-Reggiano.

(Continued)

MELTED ANCHOVIES

Makes 1½ cups

1 cup extra-virgin olive oil

100 grams peeled whole garlic cloves, crushed

200 grams salted anchovy fillets, rinsed, soaked, and deboned, or high quality anchovies packed in olive oil, drained

You get really deep flavor by letting the garlic and anchovies cook low and slow in the oil for nearly an hour. Look for deep, dark caramelization, which translates to maximum flavor. Once the garlic is soft, mash it into the oil until it completely breaks down. Make more than you need for the Cavolini or Bitter Greens and Anchovy (see page 233) pies so you can also use it to start braises, soups, or pasta sauces, or just for dipping bread or raw vegetables.

You want the consistency to be thick enough to slowly drop off a spoon but not quite spreadable.

Heat the olive oil and garlic in a small pot over medium heat. Once the cloves start to take on a bit of color, about 5 minutes, add the anchovies. Cook, breaking the anchovies up with the back of a spoon, until the fillets are melted into the oil and the garlic is deeply tender, about 40 minutes. Mash the garlic. Remove from the heat and set aside to cool. The melted anchovies will keep in a sealed container in the refrigerator for 5 days.

MAPLE BACON

Makes 1 pizza

Dough for 1 round 12-inch pizza from any of the doughs in Part 3 (page 139)

100 grams fresh mozzarella, torn or cut into 1-inch pieces

2 strips bacon, cooked 75 percent of the way and cut into ¾-inch pieces

2 tablespoons Caramelized Onions (recipe below)

1 teaspoon high quality maple syrup

This pizza is an undeniable crowd pleaser and really takes me back to my early teens when sweet and savory bacon dishes were all the rage. We like to keep the sweetness in check and only use a teaspoon of maple syrup for the whole pizza, which is enough to contrast the savoriness of the bacon without being cloying. Use the best syrup you can get your hands on.

Stretch the dough as outlined in the Techniques chapter. Transfer to a floured peel.

Distribute the mozzarella over the pizza dough to the edge of the raised border followed by the bacon and onions. Drizzle with the syrup.

Bake as directed on page 111.

Serve immediately.

CARAMELIZED ONIONS

Makes 1 cup

¼ cup plus 2 tablespoons pork fat from Pork Broth (page 226) or butter or extra-virgin olive oil

6 medium onions, thinly sliced

Sea salt

These deeply cooked onions make an appearance on quite a few pizzas other than the Maple Bacon, including the Corn Pie (page 181), Pork Pie (page 224), and Pam Yung's Bloody Butcher Polenta and Bitter Greens Pizza (page 239).

Heat the pork fat and onions in a large pan over low heat. Season with salt. Cook until soft and caramelized, about 45 minutes. The caramelized onions will keep in a sealed container in the refrigerator for 3 days.

PORK PIE

Makes 1 pizza

Dough for 1 round 12-inch pizza from any of the doughs in Part 3 (page 139)

¼ cup broth from Pork Broth and Cooked Pork (page 226), chilled, gelatinized, and cut into ½-inch cubes; plus 2 ounces cooked pork, cut into ¾-inch cubes

¼ cup Caramelized Onions (page 223)

30 grams (about 1 ounce) finely grated Parmigiano-Reggiano, plus more for dusting

Extra-virgin olive oil

A few years back, one of our favorite local farmers had some extra pig's feet. We wanted to support him as much as possible so we bought all of them and started playing around with the idea of gelatinized pork broth as a pizza topping. As you could logically conclude, I had been eating a lot of xiaolongbao, soup dumplings, at the time. They are made by enclosing pork meat and a cube of gelatinized pork broth in dough, then steaming, causing the broth to melt and fill the dumpling with hot savory deliciousness. As pizza makers, we are always looking for creative ways to moisten and weigh down the surface of the pizza to prevent it from puffing up—cheese, tomato sauce, and cream are our usual go-tos—and cubes of the rich chilled broth seemed like a fun alternative. They melt and mingle with the grated Parmigiano-Reggiano as the pizza bakes, resulting in a thickened sauce rather than a soupy topping.

Stretch the dough as outlined in the Techniques chapter. Transfer to a floured peel.

Distribute the cubed pork broth over the pizza dough to the edge of the raised border followed by the pork, onions, and Parmigiano-Reggiano. Drizzle with olive oil.

Bake as directed on page 111.

Sprinkle over additional Parmigiano-Reggiano and serve immediately.

(Continued)

When I say ¼ cup of pork broth, I mean it. If you eyeball it and use more than that, the broth will leave too much liquid on your pie.

PORK BROTH AND COOKED PORK

Makes 2 quarts broth
plus 1 to 2 cups pork

**2 pig's feet, or 3 to 4
pounds of any bone-in,
skin-on pork product**

½ onion

1 carrot

4 grams salt

3 quarts water

This process yields gelatinized pork broth, pork fat, and foot meat. We like to use pig's feet but you can use any pork product that has skin, meat, and bone, preferably from the foot, neck, or head.

In a large pot, combine the feet, onion, carrot, salt, and water.

Bring to a boil over high heat. Reduce the heat and simmer, skimming off the scum and discarding it after the first hour. Simmer until the pork is falling off the bone, about 4 hours.

Strain the broth. Pick the meat off the pig's feet and refrigerate. Cool the strained broth, cover, and store in the refrigerator overnight. You will be left with a layer of pork fat (skim it off and use for preparing Caramelized Onions, page 223, or even grilled cheese) and gelatinized pork broth that can be cubed and placed onto the pizza dough.

A key element to a successful Pork Pie is keeping the pork broth cold and solid until just before it goes on the pizza. Store it in the refrigerator until the last possible moment or it will melt.

MEATBALL

Makes 1 pizza

Dough for 1 round 12-inch pizza from any of the doughs in Part 3 (page 139)

Scant ¼ cup Tomato Sauce (page 243)

50 to 60 grams fresh mozzarella, torn or cut into 1-inch pieces

2 (1½-ounce) Meatballs (recipe follows), torn into ½- to ¾-inch pieces

¼ cup grated scamorza or low moisture mozzarella

Finely grated Pecorino Romano or Parmigiano-Reggiano

We serve meatballs as a side dish at the restaurant, and for years we had requests from regulars to put them on a pizza. In the fall of 2020, we finally did and our guests went nuts. The chorus of "what took you so long" was deafening. When torn into small pieces, the topping works really well and is certainly decadent but not too heavy. At first I was skeptical about putting something as substantial as a meatball on a pie, but I tried it for two reasons: I wanted to figure out a way to give guests a pizza they wanted without weighing down the crust; and I wanted to share our meatball recipe, which so many have asked for, so it can be enjoyed at home whether you're making pizza or not.

Stretch the dough as outlined in the Techniques chapter. Transfer to a floured peel.

Spoon the tomato sauce over the pizza dough to the edge of the raised border, then distribute the mozzarella, meatballs, scamorza, and Pecorino Romano evenly.

Bake as directed on page 111.

Sprinkle over additional Pecorino Romano and serve immediately.

(Continued)

MEATBALL

Makes about 20
meatballs

Extra-virgin olive oil

**4 cups (275 grams) day-old
country/artisan bread,
crusts removed, cut into
½-inch pieces**

2 cups milk or buttermilk

1 pound ground pork

1 pound ground beef

1 medium onion, minced

**⅓ cup Tomato Sauce (page
243)**

2 large eggs

**½ cup finely grated
Parmigiano-Reggiano**

**3 grams (½ teaspoon)
kosher salt**

**½ teaspoon freshly ground
black pepper**

I never just make two meatballs, so as long as you are preparing them for pizza, you might as well make a proper batch. You can roast the meatballs in a wood burning oven, too.

Preheat the oven to 450°F. Prepare a parchment lined baking sheet. Oil lightly.

Combine the bread and milk in a large bowl and set aside to soak.

Meanwhile, combine the pork, beef, onion, tomato sauce, eggs, Parmigiano-Reggiano, salt, and pepper in a large bowl. Gently squeeze out any excess liquid from the bread mixture so the bread is not dripping but is thoroughly moistened. Fold in the meat mixture.

Form the mixture into loose balls approximately the size of a golf ball and transfer to the prepared baking sheet.

Roast until deeply caramelized on the outside and cooked through on the inside, 20 to 25 minutes. The cooled meatballs will keep in a sealed container in the refrigerator for 4 days or in the freezer for up to 3 months.

BITTER GREENS AND ANCHOVY

Makes 1 pizza

Dough for 1 round 12-inch pizza from any of the doughs in Part 3 (page 139)

100 grams fresh mozzarella, torn or cut into 1-inch pieces

1 cup (1 recipe) Sautéed Bitter Greens (recipe below)

2 salted anchovy fillets, rinsed, soaked, and deboned, or high quality anchovies packed in olive oil, drained and cut into small pieces

5 cloves Garlic Confit (page 249)

Chili Oil (page 247)

Lemon wedge

We love the bitter and savory combination of dandelion greens, which are delivered in big bunches starting in early spring, and salted anchovies, a fundamental pantry staple in my kitchen. The two are joined in popular dishes in southern Italy so this flavor pairing really brings me back to the fragrant and fertile interior of Campania inland from Naples. You can use any bitter greens you want, but we love mixing dandelion greens and wild chicory.

Stretch the dough as outlined in the Techniques chapter. Transfer to a floured peel.

Distribute the mozzarella, greens, anchovies, and garlic over the pizza dough to the edge of the raised border.

Bake as directed on page 111.

Serve immediately with chili oil drizzled over and the wedge of lemon in the middle.

SAUTÉED BITTER GREENS

Makes 1 cup

2 tablespoons extra-virgin olive oil

2 bunches bitter greens (I like dandelion greens), roughly chopped

Sea salt, sparingly

Taste the greens before cooking to see if the stems are woody. If totally tender, leave them on. If not, strip the leaves from the stems, chop the stems finely, and add them to the pan before the leaves. Salt very sparingly as the anchovies are already very salty.

Heat the olive oil in a large pan over medium-low heat. Add the greens, season with salt, increase the heat to medium, and cook until tender, about 15 minutes.

AN HOMAGE TO ELIZABETH FALKNER'S FENNEL PIZZA

Makes 1 pizza

Dough for 1 round 12-inch pizza from any of the doughs in Part 3 (page 139)

½ cup grated Gruyère

¼ cup Roasted Fennel (recipe follows)

¼ cup Shaved Fennel (recipe follows)

¼ cup raw Sausage Mix (page 211)

Fennel fronds, picked

Pinch of fennel pollen

Elizabeth Falkner is one of the most talented chefs I have ever seen in action and it was an incredible honor to host her for a pop-up at Razza in 2019. She blew us all away with a fennel pizza that used the bulb, stalks, and fronds in a way that was so masterful, each part contributing its own texture and flavor and harmonizing perfectly. She used only Swiss cheeses, showing me and the guests that Gruyère might be one of the best pizza cheeses of all time. The recipe that follows is a tribute to the fennel pie she made that night; I add fennel sausage, too, for a heartier outcome. Vegetarians can omit it. You'll need one bulb of fennel for the recipe. To prepare, slice the bulb crosswise, separating the upper part of the bulb and stalks from the lower part of the bulb. Reserve the lower part for the roasted fennel, the upper part for the shaved fennel, and the fronds for topping the pizza.

Stretch the dough as outlined in the Techniques chapter. Transfer to a floured peel.

Distribute the Gruyère, roasted fennel, shaved fennel, and sausage over the pizza dough to the edge of the raised border.

Bake as directed on page 111.

Sprinkle over the fronds and pollen and serve immediately.

(Continued)

ROASTED FENNEL

Makes ½ cup

1 lower bulb of fennel, diced into ¼- to ½-inch cubes

Extra-virgin olive oil

Sea salt

Freshly ground black pepper

Preheat the oven to 400°F.

In a small roasting dish, combine the fennel and enough olive oil to coat. Season with salt and pepper. Cover and roast until the fennel is cooked through, about 30 minutes. Uncover and cook until caramelized, about 15 minutes more.

SHAVED FENNEL

Makes ¼ cup

INGREDIENTS	COOK'S PERCENTAGES
Fennel	100%
Salt	0.5%

Upper part of 1 fennel bulb and its stalk

0.5% sea salt

Extra-virgin olive oil

Squeeze of lemon

Shave the upper part of the bulb and stalk to 1- to 1.5-millimeter thickness with a mandoline. Weigh the fennel. Season with 0.5 percent salt by weight. Drizzle over olive oil and a squeeze of lemon and toss to combine.

PAM YUNG'S BLOODY BUTCHER POLENTA AND BITTER GREENS PIZZA

Makes 1 pizza

Dough for 1 round 12-inch pizza from any of the doughs in Part 3 (page 139)

100 grams fresh mozzarella, torn or cut into 1-inch pieces

½ cup Sautéed Bitter Greens (page 233)

2 tablespoons Caramelized Onions (page 223)

½ cup cooked polenta (recipe follows), crumbled

Freshly grated Parmigiano-Reggiano

Coarse sea salt

Extra-virgin olive oil

Back in the spring of 2019, Razza collaborated with chef Pam Yung on a pizza party to celebrate the release of Katie Parla's cookbook *Food of the Italian South*. Pam is one of the most creative humans on earth, so no one was surprised when she made a mind-blowing pizza inspired by a classic dish from the rural region of Molise featuring polenta and bitter greens. Her choice for the polenta was Bloody Butcher cornmeal, which brings an earthy sweetness, but you can use any type you wish, even leftovers.

Stretch the dough as outlined in the Techniques chapter. Transfer to a floured peel.

Distribute the mozzarella, greens, onions, and polenta over the pizza dough to the edge of the raised border. Dust with Parmigiano-Reggiano. Season with salt and drizzle with olive oil.

Bake as directed on page 111.

Drizzle with more olive oil and serve immediately.

(Continued)

POLENTA

Makes 3 cups

4 cups water

1 cup heirloom or coarse ground cornmeal (I like Bloody Butcher)

Fine sea salt

Prepare the polenta in advance so it has plenty of time to set and cool. Chill in the refrigerator before crumbling on your pizza. The cooking time will depend on the variety of corn and the freshness of the cornmeal. You'll have a lot left over if you just make the polenta for one pizza, so I recommend eating polenta for a meal and making pizza with the leftovers.

Bring a large pot of water to a boil over high heat. Season with salt. Whisk in the cornmeal, reduce the heat to low, and simmer, stirring frequently, until cooked through and tender, 1 to 3 hours. Set aside to cool.

TOMATO SAUCES

Some recipes specifically reference high or low moisture tomato sauce, while others call for fresh tomato sauce. In all cases, prepare the sauce according to the recipes that follow, then adjust based on the results of your Test Pie (see page 171). Assess whether the sauce needs more or less moisture and customize accordingly. Eventually you will be able to eyeball whether a standard tomato sauce needs to have water added or to be drained. This comes with experience. The recipes make enough sauce for 10 to 14 (12-inch) round pizzas.

TOMATO SAUCE

Makes 3½ cups

1 (28-ounce) can whole peeled tomatoes

Fine sea salt

This is the simplest sauce and the brand of tomatoes you choose should be the winner of the Tomato Evaluation Rubric (page 53). They should taste delicious with sweetness and acidity.

Analyze the texture of the tomatoes. Crush very delicate tomato brands by hand. Pass all others through a food mill. Season with fine sea salt to taste.

HIGH MOISTURE TOMATO SAUCE

For pizzas that don't bake with toppings other than tomato sauce, such as the Rossa (page 173) or Burrata (page 178), add 1 tablespoon of water to the Tomato Sauce above and stir to incorporate. Bake on a Test Pie. If the consistency is right, don't add more water. If the sauce over-reduces in the oven, mix another tablespoon of water to the sauce before building the next pizza.

LOW MOISTURE TOMATO SAUCE

For pizzas like the Jersey Margherita (page 177) that call for a slightly less viscous sauce, separate the tomato juice and the whole tomatoes and set the juice aside. Analyze the texture of the tomatoes. Crush very delicate tomato brands by hand. Pass all others through a food mill. Season with fine sea salt to taste. Bake on a Test Pie. If the sauce over-reduces during a test bake, add 2 tablespoons of the tomato juice to the sauce before building the next pizza.

FRESH TOMATO SAUCE

Makes about 4½ cups

INGREDIENT	COOK'S PERCENTAGES
Tomato	100%
Salt	0.75%

3 pounds ripe tomatoes (I like Early Girl and red or yellow plum tomatoes)

Fine sea salt

Only use fresh tomatoes in the peak of their season. I tend to stay away from heirloom tomatoes, which typically have a very high water content. You can certainly use them, though you will have to drain off some of the liquid with a fine mesh sieve.

Core the tomatoes and remove any blemishes. Cut into 1-inch pieces, then pass through a food mill. Weigh the sauce, then add 0.75 percent salt by weight and stir to dissolve.

CONDIMENTS

CHILI OIL

Makes 2 cups

60 grams mixed whole dried chilis, stems removed (I like guajillo, pasilla, and peperoncini)

2 cups neutral oil (canola or grapeseed)

The dried chili flake shaker is a standard at pizzerias in New Jersey, but we go another route and offer chili oil to guests who want a little heat. Capsaicin, the spicy compound found in chili peppers, is fat soluble, so when it's steeped in oil, its flavors really permeate. We have gone through a bunch of oil iterations over the years and have found blending two or more types of dried chilis results in a more complex oil.

I like to drizzle chili oil on any pizza that's not too fatty (so I might hold back on the Pepperoni Pizza, page 200, which is already quite unctuous), but it's great with pretty much any dark leafy green and vegetables in general. Drizzle the oil onto pizzas after they have baked; cooking dulls its impact.

Preheat the oven to 400°F.

Line a half-sheet pan with parchment and spread out the chilis evenly. Toast until fragrant, about 10 minutes.

Transfer the toasted chilis to a food processor. Pour over just enough oil for the chilis to blend. Buzz on high until the mixture has the consistency of a paste, scraping down the sides if necessary.

Transfer the paste to a small pot, add the remaining oil, and heat over medium until bubbles form, stirring occasionally. Reduce the heat to medium-low and cook until the flavors are fully extracted, 20 to 30 minutes. Set aside to cool.

Strain into a clean jar, discarding the chili solids. The oil will keep in a sealed container at room temperature for 6 weeks.

FERMENTED CHILI SAUCE

Makes 3 cups

Fermented Chili Sauce is mildly spicy, pleasantly acidic, and a perfect foil to pizza toppings that are sweet or lack acid, like the Corn Pie (page 181). The time it takes to prepare chili sauce depends on your room temperature, the kind of chilis you use, their freshness, the fermentation container, and your personal preferences. I recommend you start tasting the chilis once they have fermented for 7 days. If you like them as they are, you can use them immediately, but if you prefer a deeper flavor, ferment for up to 10 days, tasting daily. You'll get more acidity the longer you ferment, but even after 4 days you should taste some acidity, see some bubbles in the brine, and note that the chilis have softened.

Use weight rather than volume measurements for the ingredients to guarantee the fermentation proceeds correctly. Use any peppers you like.

FOR THE BRINE:

INGREDIENT	QUANTITY	COOK'S PERCENTAGES
Water	1000 grams	100%
Salt	40 grams	4%

FOR THE CHILIS:

INGREDIENT	QUANTITY	COOK'S PERCENTAGES
Red chili peppers, stems removed (I like Fresnos, long hots, or any medium-heat chili)	300 grams	100%
Red wine vinegar or white vinegar	48 grams	16%
Whole garlic cloves	10 grams	3%
Salt	1.5 grams	0.5%
Neutral oil	48 grams	16%

Prepare the Brine: Bring the water to a boil over high heat. Add the salt and stir to dissolve. Set aside to cool.

Prepare the Chilis: Pack the chilis in a large jar, fermentation crock, or a jar with an airlock. Pour over the brine to cover. If necessary, use something to weigh down the chilis so they stay fully submerged. Cover the jar with a clean kitchen towel, cheesecloth, or airlock and set aside to ferment for 7 to 10 days, tasting for doneness beginning on the fourth day. Once ready, drain and discard the brine.

Transfer the chilis to a food processor. Add the vinegar, garlic, salt, and oil and grind until smooth. Pass through a sieve or food mill. Discard the seeds and skins and transfer the chili sauce to a container with a lid. The fermented chili sauce will keep in a sealed container in the refrigerator for up to 2 weeks.

GARLIC·CONFIT

Makes 1 cup

**3 heads garlic, cloves
separated and peeled**

Extra-virgin olive oil

Who doesn't love roasted garlic? The texture is soft and melty, and the flavors are sweet and savory. I could eat so much it's obscene—so if you're like me, you will want to scale this recipe up considerably so you have lots of leftover soft garlic after using it on your pizza. Try smearing on toast, sautéing with vegetables, or serving alongside roasted chicken. Garlic confit is a nice alternative for vegetarians to use instead of the melted anchovies on the Cavolini (page 218). Store the oil separately and drizzle over raw or cooked vegetables.

Place the garlic cloves in a small pot with olive oil to cover. Heat over medium until the oil begins to bubble. Reduce the heat to low and cook until the garlic is caramelized and meltingly tender, about 1 hour. Cool and transfer to a container with a lid.

The garlic will keep for up to 1 week in a sealed container in a refrigerator.

SPRING PESTO

Makes 2 cups

2 cups packed mixed spring greens (I like garlic mustard, green onions, green garlic, ramps, or blanched stinging nettles)

Juice of ½ lemon

5 grams salt

1 cup extra-virgin olive oil

½ cup neutral oil (such as canola, grapeseed, or safflower)

50 grams finely grated Parmigiano-Reggiano

Basil is great on pizza. By extension, so is pesto. As much as I love the classic Genovese-style blend of basil, garlic, oil, pine nuts, and cheese, I like to mix it up. Recently I have been freestyling and letting my garden herbs guide me. I'll pick a bouquet of herbs and even wild greens and make a pesto that perfectly encapsulates the season. You can really make pesto all year long, depending on what herbs and greens are in season. In the winter, I will use chicory, baby spinach, or even onion grass from my yard. Feel free to do the same and make the pesto your own.

In a food processor, combine the greens, lemon juice, and salt and slowly drizzle in the olive oil and neutral oil, blending until the pesto comes together. Stir in the Parmigiano-Reggiano. The pesto will keep in an airtight container in the refrigerator for 3 days.

RESOURCES

INGREDIENTS

Alle-Pie
allepiasalumi.com
Small batch, handcrafted Italian cured meats, including guanciale, from California's central coast.

Bianco DiNapoli
biancodinapoli.com
Top notch domestic producer of vine-ripened, certified organic whole canned tomatoes.

Cairnspring Mills
cairnspring.com
Millers of fresh flour from Pacific Northwest grains.

Caputo Brothers Creamery
caputobrotherscreamery.com
Italian-style artisan cheese and mozzarella curd makers in Pennsylvania.

Castle Valley Mill
castlevalleymill.com
Freshly milled flour from heirloom wheat and Bloody Butcher cornmeal.

Central Milling
centralmilling.com
Premium flour and grains for passionate bakers.

Cherry Grove Farm
cherrygrovefarm.com
Farmstead cheeses from grass-fed raw cow's milk.

Corto
corto-olive.com
Quality extra-virgin olive oil for wholesale.

Farmer Ground Flour
farmergroundflour.com
Fresh, stoneground flour from New York State organic grain.

The Foraged Feast
theforagedfeast.com
Purveyor of locally and sustainably sourced mushrooms, greens, herbs, and more.

Gustiamo
gustiamo.com
Importer of the finest Italian foods including whole canned tomatoes (like Gustarosso brand), salted anchovies, and extra-virgin olive oil.

Jersey Girl Cheese
jerseygirlcheese.com
Fresh and aged Italian-style cheeses and ricotta made in northern New Jersey.

King Arthur Baking Company
kingarthurbaking.com
Widely available, extremely reliable, unbleached flour.

Lesaffre
lesaffreyeast.com
The industry standard for instant yeast; all yeasted recipes in the book were developed with the company's Saf-Instant yeast.

The Meadow

themeadow.com
Portland-based sea salt specialists and purveyor of stellar imported pantry items.

Stanislaus

stanislaus.com
California-based tomato canners supplying restaurants. Retail consumers can find their Alta Cucina tomatoes online.

Tempesta Artisan Salumi

tempestaartisansalumi.com
Producer of exceptional guanciale and other cured meats.

EQUIPMENT

Baking Steel

bakingsteel.com
Carbon steel baking surfaces for fast and efficient heat transfer.

DoughMate

doughmate.com
Sells a wide assortment of dough proofing boxes for professionals; some even fit in the home refrigerator!

Gi.Metal

gimetalusa.com
Pizza peels, oven brushes, and other useful tools for making pizza.

LloydPans

lloydpans.com
My preferred square pans for baking pizza, made in Washington State.

Mockmill

mockmill.us
Tabletop mills for making flour at home.

Pizza Resource Center

pizzaresourcecenter.com
Online store for pizza making tools, books, and gear.

Pleasant Hill Grain

pleasanthillgrain.com
Nebraska-based store specializing in kitchen equipment including Famag spiral mixers, tabletop flour mills, dough proofers, and pizza tools.

HIGH TEMPERATURE OVENS

Breville

breville.com
The Breville Pizzaiolo is an electric oven that can be used indoors.

Forza Forni

forzaforni.com
Importer of Acunto and Pavesi wood fired ovens from Italy and designer of custom pizza projects.

Gozney

gozney.com
Roccbox and Dome outdoor wood and gas fired pizza ovens for home and commercial use.

Mugnaini

mugnaini.com
Valoriani outdoor wood fired oven kits and portable and preassembled ovens for home and commercial use.

Ooni

ooni.com
Portable pizza ovens for outdoor use.

VIDEOS AND PDFs

Pizza Evaluation Rubric

Tomato Evaluation Rubric

Olive Oil Evaluation Rubric

Mozzarella Evaluation Rubric

Scissor Pinch Method

Rubaud Method

Envelope Fold

Coil Fold

Divide and Round

Stretch a Round Pizza

Transfer Pizza to a Peel

Launch the Round Pizza (Home Oven)

Stretch a Pan Pizza

Load the Oven (High Temp)

ACKNOWLEDGMENTS

I owe a debt of gratitude to the pizza makers who came before me and who slowly changed people's expectations of what pizza should be. I don't think my pizza, which is so different from the pizza of my youth, would have been received with the same enthusiasm if there wasn't already a conversation decades in the making pushing pizza dough and toppings to new heights.

To all of my pizza pals across the country, I've learned so much from all of you, and I hope you enjoy this book and see it as a representation of the love we share for pizza and our industry.

To my wife, Nicole, you nurture our family and our lives with such grace, elegance, and kindness. You are a role model for us, and I'm endlessly grateful for your love and support. Alexandra and Elliot—you fill our lives with eternal joy; I pray one day you experience the joy and love that you bring your mother and me.

Katie Parla, thank you for your friendship and support over the past decade. When I decided I was ready to write a book, you were my very first phone call. You have held my hand through the entire process, and there's no one on earth who would have been a better book partner than you. This book would not exist without you.

To my teammates at Razza, past and present: I have learned so much from all of you and YOU are what make Razza a magical place. Your genuine care for one another and for our guests is simply inspiring. Thank you for allowing me the time and space to be a husband and a father first. Thank you in particular to Nick Malaspina, Joe Trembley, and Clint Ives for leading our kitchen team with kindness and for helping with recipe development and testing. Thank you to Octavio and Jonah for your constant attention to the intricate details of dough making and dough management. Thank you to our pizza team—Margerito, Alfredo, Ever, Sergio, and Nelson. You impress me every day, and I am forever grateful for your hard work, dedication, and loyalty. A huge thank you to Carina Clores, Stretch, and Kevin D for all that you've done for our culture at Razza and for bringing so much joy to our guests over the past few years. Thank you to Stephanie Rizzolo for all that you do. Thank you to Kevin Mahan for helping me climb out of one of life's many valleys. A special thank you to my cousin Kevin Richer for the endless support, leadership, and wisdom at Razza and in life.

Thank you to my agent, David Black, for taking me on as a client and for the support and guidance along the way. Thank you, Michael Szczerban and the whole Voracious team, for believing in this book and making it all happen—including Ben Allen, Nyamekye Waliyaya, Thea Diklich-Newell, Jessica Chun, Stephanie Reddaway, Lauren Ortiz, Deri Reed, and many more. Thank you to Katie Shelly for your beautiful illustrations that bring abstract concepts to life. Thank you to Eric Wolfinger for your friendship, guidance, and creativity. Thank you to Izzy, Spencer, and Eric's wife, Alma, for letting him shoot the book nearly up to the minute of giving birth. Thank you to Seton Rossini for your gorgeous cover design, and to Shubhani Sarkar for the amazing interior! Thank you to Li Wang for a serendipitous partnership and for help with thejoyofpizzabook.com

Thank you to flour genius Kevin Morse and tomato royalty Rob DiNapoli for your generous and thought-provoking conversations. Thank you to my friends at Stanislaus and Corto Olive Oil for sharing your wisdom and always being available to talk through my nerdy queries. Grazie mille to Sal Pisani and the team from Jersey Girl Cheese.

Thank you to Jo Ann Parla, Peter Dejong and the Forza Forni crew, Didier Rosada, David Garci-Aguirre, Tom Cortopassi, Steve Rouse, Jeff Yankellow, Scott Wiener, Mark and Jenny Bello, and Dr. Tom Molnar. Thank you to Ethan Frisch and the team at Burlap & Barrel for sourcing and blending chilies for us! Thank you to Jono Pandolfi for crafting a gorgeous and functional pizza plate for us. Thank you to Dan Lipow for your friendship and your glorious wild edibles. Thank you to the Giglio family for inviting me into your lives and for Lucia's lessons on eggplant and tomatoes.

Thank you to our landlords, Eric and Paul Silverman. You and your team are a dream to work with. We're grateful for all of your support on a daily basis.

Jersey City, you are one of a kind. Thank you to our neighbors and guests for keeping our restaurant open since 2012. We are grateful to be a part of this community and we hope we're making you proud.

Thank you to all of the families who have entrusted me with your pizza nights and family celebrations over the past two decades. We have been through so much together! Thank you for allowing me into your families and for supporting my journey. Thank you to Chris and Jack Santi for believing in me and giving me the confidence to become a small business owner at such a young age. Thank you to Sue G and Sue T for your support in the earliest days of my career. Thank you to Don Savoy! Thank you to Josh Friedland and Robin and Sue for your kindness and creativity.

A huge thank you to all of the journalists who have helped tell our stories over the years. We would not be writing this book without your hard work and dedication to your craft.

My brother Seth has taught me many things in life. Thanks in particular for teaching me about rubrics in 2007. This book wouldn't exist without you and your loving support. Thanks for being the best human I know.

Thank you to all of my aunts, uncles, and cousins for always being there for me. I love you all. Thank you to Phyllis and Jerry Jones for your endless encouragement and for believing that one day this would happen. Thank you to the entire Sabel Family!

Thank you to my mom and dad for equipping me with the tools necessary to navigate life. I wish you were here to see this.

INDEX

ABOUT
THE AUTHORS

DAN RICHER is the chef and owner of Razza in Jersey City. A graduate of Rutgers University, he skipped his own graduation to fly to Italy and begin his real education: in pizza. He is a four-time semifinalist for the James Beard Foundation's Best Chef: Mid-Atlantic award, and a James Beard Rising Star Chef semifinalist. The *New York Times* has called his pizza the best in New York—and it's served in New Jersey. Visit Dan at Razza in Jersey City and follow him @razzanj and @danricher.

KATIE PARLA is an Italy-based food and beverage writer, culinary guide, educator, and award-winning cookbook author. She is the cohost of the *Gola* podcast about Italian food and culture and regularly appears as an Italy expert on CNN, the Travel Channel, and the History Channel. Her self-titled cooking and travel programs appear on Recipe.TV. She has lived in Rome since 2003 and Razza is always her first stop when visiting her home state of New Jersey from Italy. Keep up with Katie @katieparla.